NATLAND
and Oxenhome

The story of a Westmorland Village

Winifred Inglesfield

Published by
H E L M
PRESS

With acknowledgement to the assistance
of the Curwen Archive Trust

Dedicated to Natlanders past and present.

Published by Helm Press
10 Abbey Gardens, Natland, Kendal, Cumbria LA9 7SP
Tel: 015395 61321
E.mail: **helmpress@ktdbroadband.com**

First published 2006

Typeset in Berkley Old Style

ISBN 0 9550823 3 1
978 0 9550823 3 7

Typeset and printed by Stramongate Press, Canal Head, Kendal

Front cover: St. Mark's Church, Natland

Back cover: Natland Palm Fair 1810 in appliqué. Made by Whin.

Contents

Whin on Loughrigg

INTRODUCTION

... to be aware if you like that one is part of an immense unbroken stream that has flowed over this scene for more than a thousand years: but at rate to look at every feature with exact knowledge, able to give a name to it and knowing how it got there, and not just to gaze uncomprehendingly at it as a beautiful but silent view.

W.G. Hoskins, *Provincial England: Essays in Social and Economic History* (London: Macmillan, 1963), p. 228.

Which is why I put this little book together. Any errors can only be blamed on myself – and old age. You can check and enlarge on the information at the Kendal Record Office. When the Women's Institute celebrated its fifty years – 1919-1969 – members were asked to record how the village had changed over that period. It certainly had changed. Mrs Lavinia Swainbank wrote the record for Oxenholme, and I did the same for Natland – and the research that this involved provided the basis for the present book.

I wish to thank all those who have helped me – the staff of the Westmorland County Archives (now the Kendal branch of Cumbria County Archives), and, in particular, former County Archivist Sheila MacPherson and, more recently, Richard Hall; Anne Bonney, who guided me through the hoops of production, helping and encouraging me; and my family, who, as always, helped me and kept me going. Wendy Balmer kindly lent her copy of Blezard's 'Original Westmorland Songs,' and a host of others gave advice and information, and provided photos – Stan O'Connor, Graham Needham, John Marsh, Percy Duff, Barbara Nelson, Philip Ball, John Atkinson, Ingrid Beattie, Rhian Peters, Pat and Robert Dodgson, and Mavis and Bill Moffat. Mrs Mary Juel-Jensen gave permission to reproduce photos taken by her mother, Mrs E. Maples. The Editor of the *Westmorland Gazette* gave permission to use some of their old photos, and Kendal Library actually produced copies – all very helpful. Many years ago I was able to thank dear old Mrs Pooley Nelson, who knew so much of the old Natland. You have all helped and cheered me along the way.

I'd like to think that Natland will always be a village, and never become part of Kendal!

Whin Inglesfield.

Whin Inglesfield, June 2006

1

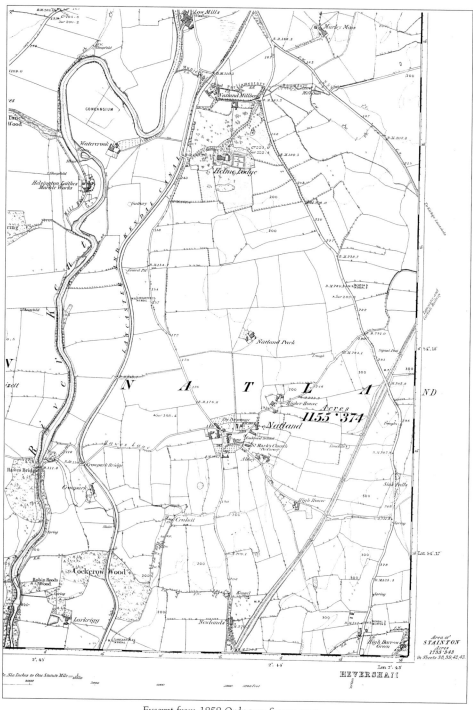

Excerpt from 1858 Ordnance Survey map

Courtesy Kendal Record Office

2

Chapter 1

THE VILLAGE AND ITS ORIGINS

THE LIE OF THE LAND

Natland village lies about a mile south of the Kendal Borough boundary, in the former County of Westmorland, now part of Cumbria. On March 31st 1974, when some of the county boundaries were altered, the counties of Cumberland and Westmorland, Lancashire North of the Sands, and part of the West Riding of Yorkshire, were merged to form the new County of Cumbria – Cumbria again after 1026 years! Natland itself lies about five miles north of the Lancashire border, as the crow flies.

In 1691 the Rev. Thomas Machell, the Rector of Kirkby Thore, toured South Westmorland on horseback. He hired a guide and set off to Natland, where, he tells us in his writings, 'there was a little chapel lately rebuilt and a delicate level green with houses about it, of which three or four are very good houses.'

Another person of note who visited Natland even earlier than Machell was the poet Richard Brathwaite (his name was spelt variously) of Burneside. Brathwaite was a man of some learning, who wrote both Latin and English doggerel, his most famous poem being reprinted as 'Drunken Barnaby's Journal.' His interest in Natland seems to have been restricted to a particular young woman:

> Now to Natland, where choice beauty
> And a Shepheard doe salute me,
> Lips I relish richly roseack
> Purely Nectar and Ambroseack;
> But I'm chaste, as doth become me,
> For the Countreys eyes are on me.

Today the village Green is still there, and if he were here today Machell would recognise it, in spite of many changes. There is a Church on a new site, several older houses have been modernised, a bungalow built, and three new houses have replaced the village School, which moved to a new site. The School House is now a private house. The village Green today has a road round the perimeter, and the earlier crossroads have been grassed over.

There are two trees on the Green now – a hawthorn and an oak. The hawthorn replaced a former one – and there were doubtless several before that, as a hawthorn had grown on the Green from time immemorial. The original hawthorn, which would be the native white variety, may have been planted on the site of the old preaching cross. Hawthorns were often regarded as having religious significance, the best known example being the Glastonbury thorn in Somerset. Formerly gypsies had camped on the Green: indeed, they had made Natland their headquarters, and there had been colourful and merry village fairs with dancing round the old thorn tree. Generations of Natlanders must have danced and made merry round the tree, and young lovers plighted their troth under its branches. There is even a song about these activities, 'Bonny Jane of Natland.' The oak tree, given by Norman and Molly Croft, was brought from Windsor Great Park to celebrate the Coronation of Queen Elizabeth II in 1953. The oak was planted by two boys of Natland School – Carter Croft and Christopher Crewdson. A TV set was hired for the occasion – with a large screen, something very new for most of us. There are now two seats on the Green. The one nearest to the Church gate is a memorial to my husband Sam Inglesfield, who was Headmaster of Natland School from 1945 to 1956. The other seat has been placed more recently – a memorial to Pearson Charnley, who was always ready to help and advise with whatever was going on.

Roads lead off from the corners of the Green – to Kendal, Oxenholme, Sedgwick and down Hawes Lane, crossing the Kent by the ancient Hawes Bridge, to the A6. The Church dominates the Green; and beyond the Church, to the east and above the railway on its high embankment, stretches the 600 feet eminence of Helm – some prefer to call it the Helm – like a lion dormant. The lower and more distant horizon of Scout Scar dominates the view to the west, beyond the River Kent, hidden in its gorge. The green fields of Natland Park Farm lie beyond the Vicarage and the old School House, the land gently sloping away to Kendal (as viewed from the Church tower). Southwards towards Sedgwick there are more green hills and fields. From the summit of Helm the view takes in Morecambe Bay, the Lake District fells, the Howgill fells and the Lunesdale fells: on a clear day it is a magnificent view, well worth climbing up to see.

Whilst Oxenholme village lies within Natland's ecclesiastical parish, it lies within the civil parish of Kendal. The Natland boundary does a big zigzag before moving south below Barrows Green, then moving north again, avoiding the Larkrigg fields. (Larkrigg is geographically part of Natland, but joined the lands of Sizergh Castle, in Helsington Parish, about 1712.) Our western boundary then follows the river up to curve round the Roman camp at Watercrook, avoiding the Kendal sewerage works – and so back to square one. The map of Natland shows all this clearly.

Years ago I asked Richard Swainbank about the geology of Natland. Richard was born and bred at Oxenholme, attended Natland School, and became a geologist working in Canada and Alaska. Briefly – Helm is an outcrop of the Silurian rock that makes up much of the southern part of the Lake District.

The junction of the Silurian rock and Carboniferous limestone lies just where the Burton to Kendal road runs along the bottom of Helm. The limestone underlies the village and adjacent areas, and it is covered by a layer of clay laid down by glaciers that retreated some 10,000 years ago. Water drains through the limestone by a system of caves and fissures, emerging as springs here and there, particularly down by the River Kent. Some of these caves were discovered when the railway was built, as the cutting was broken through, south of Oxenholme Station. The glacial clay is responsible for the flooding of various field hollows, where in the harder winters of former years the children of Natland enjoyed sliding on the ice. And now this causes problems on building sites.

Originally Natland had 1156 acres within our boundary, including 20 acres of water – the River Kent. Now we have only 892: how did we manage to lose 264 acres? The Rural District Council kindly supplied the information. I can't do better than quote *verbatim*:

> The Oxenholme area of the civil Parish of Natland was transferred to the Borough of Kendal on April 1st, 1935. According to my information the transferred area contained 264 acres. The transfer was made as a result of a general review made by Westmorland County Council of the county districts comprising the administrative and geographical county of Westmorland. All County Councils in England and Wales were required to undertake such a review by the Local Government Act, 1929. The local reason for the transfer was that it was considered that provision should be made for expansion of the town of Kendal.

THE NAME 'NATLAND'

How did we come by the name 'Natland'? *The Place Names of Westmorland*, English Place-Name Society, 2 vols (Cambridge: Cambridge University Press, 1967), 1, gives various references to Natland over the centuries:

Natalund – 1170-80
Natalaund – 1170-80, 1190-1200, 1292
Natalunt – 1246
Natalund – 1246, 1255-72
Natalande – 1290-1312, 1426, 1452, 1657

The second element of the name is the Old Norse 'lundr,' a small wood or sacred grove. For the first element *The Place Names of Westmorland* suggests several possibilities. The Old Norse name 'Nati' occurs only as the mythological name of a giant in the Norse Edda; but there is also the possibility of Old Norse 'nata,' nettle, or a root 'nat-,' meaning wet, corresponding to the Old English 'næt.' Knowing that so many of our local names derive from Old Norse, I wrote many years ago to the Norsk Stadnamnarkiv, the Norwegian Archive of Place Names in Oslo. Their reply gave some rather different suggestions – I quote:

> I rather think we have the Old Norse 'hnot' (f), 'nut' as the first element, as in the compound 'hnataskogr,' 'nut-wood.' We have a lot of place-names as: 'Nataskogen' ('skog' – 'wood'), 'Natalundn,' 'Natalia,' all with the same ON compound 'Nata' – 'Hnata' – and with the same meaning, 'where nuts are growing.' Compare the farm name Natland near Bergen where you will still find nut trees on the hillside.

This is the photo of a street name in Bergen, 'Natlands Veien.' Hazel grows abundantly in the woods around Natland. There is, then, no single satisfactory explanation: you can take your pick.

EARLY SETTLERS

We must remember the countless generations of folk who lived, loved and died in this area. Archaeological finds prove that there have been people in these parts for a very long time. The earliest would be fisher-hunter-food gatherers, living off what they could find in the countryside. They would live in temporary shelters – or caves, if such were available. Temporary shelters rarely leave identifiable sites. These people buried their dead in quite elaborate tumuli (cairns or barrows), some of which contained several chambers; food and personal possessions were frequently deposited with the body, reflecting a belief in some kind of journey to another life. These are usually quite obvious in the countryside. Our nearest burial cairns are on Sizergh Fell and in Levens Park. They also constructed stone circles of varying size – there are several stone circles in Cumbria, the nearest being a small example on Casterton Fell in the Lune valley at OS map reference SD 640799. Many years ago this small circle was excavated and a beaker burial was found, a primitive beaker or pot containing cremated bones. The purpose of these circles is not known. Apart from the occasional burial they could have been meeting places for various functions (as we have a village hall), for tribal gatherings, and in some cases there has apparently been a connection with astronomical observation, and in particular the midsummer sunrise. These ancient peoples originated on the Continent, spreading out in waves, seeking suitable land. The earliest would be able to walk over before Britain became an island: the sea broke through some time between 8,000 and 5,000 BC. Later they would use primitive boats. They had only stone, flint and bone implements, with no knowledge of metals. There was no flint in this area, but a suitable alternative was found on the fells above Langdale – volcanic tuff, which proved to produce serviceable axes for forest clearance. Clearance can be dated, by study of the pollen grains in borings in boggy ground, to about 4,500 BC. The grains can be identified as those of plants that quickly colonise cleared land, such as ribwort plantain, docks and sorrels. Tracks would develop as people moved about, and some of those tracks may be the origin of some of our later roads. One of our Natland lanes, Helm Lane, seems to be part of an ancient track. The A685 road, coming over the moors from Tebay and Grayrigg to Kendal, has a sharp eastward turn, crossing the railway. From it branches off a fairly narrow lane, Paddy Lane (an old name), which runs along above Benson Hall and below Benson Knott, keeping on roughly the same contour and crossing the steep Greyhound hill, which climbs up from Kendal. After another stretch the lane crosses the A684 road from Kendal to Sedbergh, cutting across Helm. Bearing slightly south-south-west, it crosses the A65 Kendal to Kirkby Lonsdale road, and makes a beeline downhill to Natland. There it crosses the village Green, down past the village shop and, as Hawes Lane, winds its way down over the canal bridge, Crowpark Bridge. Before the canal bridge and Hawes Bridge were built, the lane would head directly to the ancient ford over the River Kent. Then it climbs over the hill and continues across the A6, up a lane to Brigsteer. Fairly recently a corduroy road (made of logs of wood) was discovered crossing the Lyth valley, which in past times was very boggy. From there onwards the route is not clear, as there are lanes running off in different directions.

At least 5,000 years have passed since Stone Age tribes started the lengthy process of clearance of the dense forest that would fill the Kent valley. Over many centuries wave upon wave of new peoples flowed into our country, carrying new ideas – the Bronze Age people bringing knowledge of metal working. The Stone and Bronze Age people have left plenty of evidence of their occupation elsewhere throughout the country, but little has been found, to date, in Natland itself, apart from a stone-age axe-hammer that was found at Larkrigg. This was reported in the *Transactions of the Cumberland and Westmorland Antiquarian and Archaeological Society* of 1935. It was 9 inches long, $3\frac{1}{2}$ inches broad, and 3 inches thick, with a rounded butt. This axe-hammer is in Kendal Museum. The early peoples lived in small groups of wooden huts or rough shelters, which left no trace on the landscape. Their successors, of the Iron Age, were a widespread northern tribe called the Brigantes. They were hunters and farmers, wove cloth and made pottery. What beliefs were held by these early tribes we can only guess. Some certainly believed in an after-life, as they were buried with

The Iron Age Fort on Helm

The cock-pit. The circular walled-in wood area near Appletree School. Courtesy late Mrs. Maples.

personal possessions, weapons and food, as if for a journey to another life. Surely the natural forces which affected their lives – sun, moon, stars, wind, trees, or whatever – must have made an impression on them and been objects of veneration.

The Iron Age people lived in settlements, groups of round stone huts with thatched roofs. Sometimes a central hut might be larger than the others, perhaps the home of a local chieftain. They had walled pens for their livestock, and a strong surrounding wall with a heavily protected entrance. Their small walled fields were close by. This kind of settlement persisted throughout the later centuries BC, well into the period of the Roman occupation, the later examples often being referred to as 'Romano-British settlements.' Their remains can be found mostly on higher ground where they have not been destroyed by agricultural activities. There are remains of an Iron Age settlement in Levens Park, not far from here, and such upland valleys as Kentmere have several. The remains appear as the bases of stone walls and earth banks, and are especially clear after a light fall of snow which picks out the different features. There are one or two possible hut circles on Helm, not far below the summit, identified by archaeologist Clare Fell as possibly dating back to the Iron Age. We have substantial evidence of the Iron Age in Natland: there is a typical Iron Age hill-fort on the summit of Helm, known as Castlesteads, with a flattened top, banks and ditches, all eroded by the passage of time and human feet. When the Romans arrived they used the Helm fort as a lookout. The summit of Helm now bears an Ordnance Survey column.

Two other possible archaeological sites should be mentioned. Down by the River Kent, about 16 feet above the level of the lane, on the right-hand side and just before the lane drops down to Hawes Bridge, there is a distinct mound. It is oval at the base, about 133 feet by 100 feet, and about 25 feet across the top. In spring 1972 I asked an archaeologist from the University of Newcastle-upon-Tyne, Barbara Harbottle, who had a close connection with the Cumberland and Westmorland Antiquarian and Archaeological Society, to examine this site. She arranged for the mound to be surveyed, but concluded that without a dig it was difficult to come to any firm conclusion about its origins. Perhaps it was a motte-and-bailey, an early fortification, or simply a drumlin, a relic of the Ice Age. In any case, this feature has been recorded by the University of Newcastle. The mound might have had connections with the lost Bodelforde, which was registered in the Domesday Book. According to *The Place-Names of Westmorland*, 1, p. 113, the name, which appears as 'Bothelford' in later documents, means 'the ford near the dwelling.' The exact location of this place, possibly a hamlet, is not known, though we can assume it lay on the River Kent, either in Natland or Helsington.

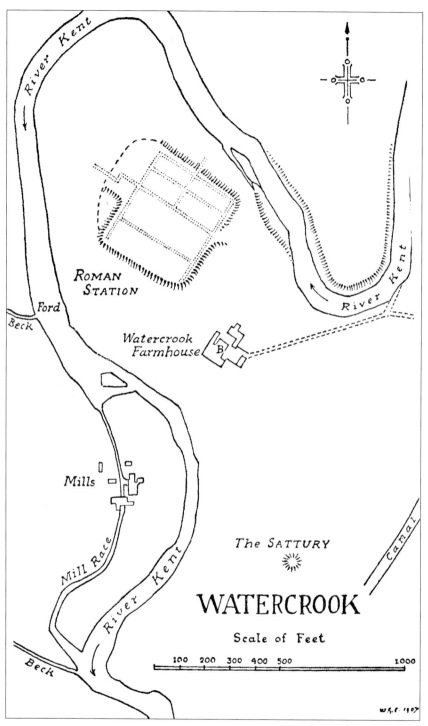

Courtesy late Mrs. Maples.

The second possible site is the small roughly circular walled-in wood near the former St Mark's Home (Appletree School). The name of the field surrounding this wood is recorded on the Corn Rent map as 'Raise,' a common place-name element, derived from the Norse 'hreysi,' meaning a cairn (see below, 'Origin of Field Names and Other Place Names'). The wood, which occupies a low hilltop, does indeed contain a large, sprawling heap of stones, once used as a cockpit, and recorded as such in the Royal Commission on Historical Monuments survey of 1936 (*An Inventory of the Historical Monuments in Westmorland* [London: HMSO, 1936], p. 180). Is it a prehistoric burial cairn or tumulus? Archaeological investigation might provide the answer. It is worth noting that the wood is close to the spring near Little Cracalt.

THE ROMANS: ALAUNA

The Romans arrived in the south in AD 43, but it was not until AD 79 or 80 that the Roman General Agricola's troops established a fort at Watercrook. This was six miles west of the main line of advance – up the western side of the Pennines via Lancaster, the Lune valley, Low Borrow Bridge near Tebay, Brougham and points north. But how did they make their way to Watercrook? Agricola must have taken another route. A few years ago a possible second route north from Lancaster, passing a small military site at Hincaster, was suggested. It may have followed the narrow lane that runs up hill and down dale from Stainton, past Low Barrows Green Farm and Newlands, continuing to present-day Natland; it is possible that it then followed the footpath that leads north from the Green towards Natland Park Farm – and so on to Watercrook. However they came, the existence of the fort at Watercrook isn't in question. Its name was 'Alauna' or its variants 'Alone,' which appears in the Antonine Itinerary, and 'Alione' (*The Place Names of Westmorland*, 1, p. 113). Alauna was established on a large meander of the River Kent, about a mile south of what is now Kendal. It originally had earth and turf embankments and wooden buildings, but these were replaced by stone structures thirty to forty years later. The fort had the normal square pattern of Roman camps; measuring 370 feet by 400 feet, it could accommodate an infantry cohort of five hundred men. There was a bathhouse, its site now occupied by Watercrook Farm. Alauna is thought to have been connected by road to the fort at Galava, near Ambleside, but so far efforts to discover evidence of such a road have been unsuccessful. One might conjecture that a road crossed the limestone ridge of Cunswick Scar, later skirting the foot of Wansfell.

Eventually a civilian settlement (a '*vicus*') developed on the east side of the fort. It originally consisted of strip houses of wood, but later the external walls were rebuilt in stone. A long clay hearth was found in one of them.

Almost certainly the local British population helped to supply meat and grain, and it is possible that some were employed in the camp itself. Finds such as brooches and other jewellery suggest a relatively affluent population in the *vicus*. A stone stamp, used as a maker's mark on pottery, suggests some manufacture. The heyday of the *vicus* was in the second century.

Alauna was recognised as a Roman fort as early as the seventeenth century; but it was in the very dry summer of 1887, when the grass covering the fortifications was parched, with the outlines of the fort clearly picked out, that its extent was first realised. Excavations in 1930-31, 1944 and 1974, uncovered many finds that greatly extended our knowledge. Pottery, including characteristic Roman Samian ware, and many coins, suggested continuous occupation to the fourth century. There were also a number of inscribed stones, one being the tombstone of an officer of the XXth Legion, carrying the warning that 'anyone putting another corpse into this grave will be fined' (this in Latin of course). That stone is in the British Museum, but Kendal Museum houses a good collection of items from Watercrook and other local sites. Even recently Roman masonry has been found as flood waters have eroded the river banks. Excavations indicate that Alauna was occupied up to and after the final evacuation of the Roman Wall at the close of the fourth century AD.

Tacitus, the Roman historian, in his biography of his father-in-law, Agricola, wrote, 'In the summer [of 79 AD] he himself chose sites for camps and reconnoitred estuaries and forts; and all the time he gave the enemy no rest, but constantly launched plundering raids.' Presumably the 'enemy' was the British tribe, the Brigantes, who occupied a wide area of northern Britain at that time. The presence of the Romans must have greatly affected the lives of the local British population. Some Roman troops doubtless married native women and settled locally, their descendants becoming absorbed into the native population. This area was part of the military zone of Britain, and cannot boast Roman villas and so on. Only the relic features of their roads and fortifications bear witness to the fact that the Roman Eagle was carried proudly over our northern hills. The Romans had an infinite variety of gods, and occasionally there is evidence of Christian belief in tombstones bearing Christian symbols.

Before we leave Watercrook Farm, I must mention a prominent mound lying about 300 yards south of the farm, and known as Sattury on the modern map; the name appears as 'Saterhowe' in a document of 1348 (*The Place Names of Westmorland*, p. 114), and as 'Sattery' in the schedule of the 1836 Kendal Corn Rent map. The mound is listed in the RCHM survey (*An Inventory of the Historical Monuments in Westmorland*, p. 182). It is oval, about 188 feet across at the widest point, and some 17 feet high. It looks an unnatural feature on the landscape, but who knows what it is without excavation? Years ago Gladys Brennand, whose brother Nat Bell lived at Watercrook Farm at one time, told me that they knew this mound as Monks' Hill, believing it to have been a monks' burial ground. Indeed, several identified burials have been found nearby.

ANGLO-SAXONS AND NORSEMEN

The years immediately following the withdrawal of the Romans have left relatively little archaeological evidence. From about 540 AD, however, there was a migration of folk from the north German plains, known to us as the Anglo-Saxons – an agricultural people seeking new lands. They followed the east coast of Britain up to what is now Northumberland, eventually spreading out westwards through the river gaps in the Pennines. This northern area of Britain, along with Wales, was part of the Kingdom of Strathclyde, governed from Dunbarton Rock on the River Clyde. The native British people called themselves 'Cymry,' from which the name Cumberland is derived (the Welsh name for Wales is 'Cymru'). The Anglo-Saxon Chronicle, which was written much later, refers to 'Westmoringaland,' meaning 'the land of the people west of the moors (the Pennines),' from which 'Westmorland' is derived. The Anglo-Saxons were concerned with raising crops, and settled on the fertile lower lands surrounding the central mountains of the Lake District, especially to the west, where they established settlements whose names contain the typical place name endings, 'ton' and 'ham.' They introduced a heavy ox-drawn plough capable of cultivating land difficult or impossible for earlier farmers to cultivate. The Anglo-Saxons dominated Cumbria for at least two hundred years.

The spread of Christianity during Anglo-Saxon times is witnessed by several beautiful sculptured crosses, a fine example of which stands proudly in the churchyard at Irton in West Cumbria. The fragment of a cross, dating from approximately 800 AD, was found during building work at Kendal Parish Church. There must have been a very early church at Kendal, as Kendal Parish Church became the mother church of a wide area, and, no doubt, established Christianity in Natland and many villages around. A document of 1312 mentions 'the cross in Nateland' (see below, 'Records of the Barony of Kendale'): of stone or wood, it doubtless stood on the village Green. Village greens are indeed typical of Anglian settlement, and our Green will have witnessed countless activities for well over a thousand years.

In the late eighth century Danish raiders caused great distress on the Northumbrian coast, challenging the Anglo-Saxon authority, but a greater threat to our area came from the west. Norsemen (Vikings) appeared in the Orkneys and Shetlands in the mid-eighth century. They spread out round the Scottish coast and through the Western Isles, eventually reaching Northern Ireland and the Isle of Man, where they doubtless intermarried with the native population. It is thought these 'Irish-Norse' carried out raids on what is now the coast of Cumbria, before actually settling in the early tenth century. They were a pastoral people who established summer settlements in the inner valleys. The name Natland is itself evidence that the Norsemen settled here, and, as we shall see, many of the older field names are Old Norse in origin. The Norse language is known to have persisted, leaving a permanent mark on the local dialect. The Norsemen were skilled craftsmen, and like their predecessors they have left a legacy of stone crosses, such as the magnificent fifteen feet high cross in Gosforth churchyard in West Cumbria. Like the Anglians they sited their houses, which would be mere huts of wood and thatch, in the most advantageous positions, with a nearby water supply and some shelter. Over the centuries these would be replaced and rebuilt, using stone and slate roofing. Indeed many present-day farmsteads have their origins in the dwellings of early Norse settlers.

NORSE WORDS IN THE LOCAL DIALECT

The Westmorland dialect, including many familiar topographical and farming terms, owes much to the language of the Norsemen (for a fascinating account of the impact of Old Norse on the languages and dialects of Britain, see John Geipel, *The Viking Legacy: The Scandinavian Influence on the English and Gaelic Languages* [Newton Abbot: David and Charles, 1971]). Among the farming terms are 'gimmer,' two-year-old ewe, and 'shippon,' cowshed, both still regularly used. 'Kist,' chest or box, 'ley,' scythe, 'rygel,' bridle, and 'sile,' sieve, were certainly used well into the last century, while 'clegg,' horse-fly, is still to be heard. 'Brant' is steep' and 'lang' is long; to 'gang' is to go, to 'ken' is to know, to 'laik' is to play, to 'lait' is to seek, and to 'lig' is to lie. 'Aik,' oak, 'brig,' bridge, 'eller,' alder, and 'stain,' stone, are all familiar from place names. 'Gowder,' echo, now only found in place names, and 'gowk,' cuckoo, are both derived directly from the Norse. My father used words such as 'girt,' great or big, 'kysty,' choosy, to 'scop,' throw, 'scowp,' a bowl-like measure, 'thrang,' busy, and 'yarking,' gaunt (often used of buildings). 'Kush-kush,' which may also have come down from Norse settlers, is a timeless cry still to be heard when cattle are being driven in for milking. My own favourite dialect phrase is 'Like an owd yow liggin' de-ad aback o't dyke,' like an old ewe lying dead behind the hedge or wall – in other words, feeling very poorly!

A remarkable survival into modern times were the old sheep-counting numerals, which differed from place to place; all versions have a strong rhythm. One version, formerly used in Borrowdale, was as follows (one to ten): 'yan, tyan, tethera, methera, pimp, sethera, lethera, hovera, dovera, dick.' The words for five and ten are almost identical to the corresponding Welsh numerals, suggesting a very ancient origin. Using the natural counting frame of the hand, the shepherds seem to have counted in fives.

ORIGIN OF FIELD NAMES AND OTHER PLACE NAMES

There are records of many old Natland field names, some of which, as we have seen, are Old Norse in origin. I quote directly from *The Place Names of Westmorland*, 1, p.114. The principal names in (a) are taken from the 1836 Corn Rent map, those in (b) from *Records Relating to the Barony of Kendal* (see Chapter 2); references are to the glossary of 'Elements of Place-Name and Field-Name Elements' in vol. 2:

(*a*)   Barrels Know; Barrows green; Birket; Brashan; Briary brow; Broad flatt (*le Bradeflatt* 1312, *v.* brād, flat); Broad mire; Buckwell park; Busky sloes; Chamber ings (cf. Chamber's Tenement i, 110 *supra*, eng); Cring ling (*v.* kringla 'circular pit,' eng); high & low Crook (*v.* krókr); Elsy bank & lane; Fitz (*v.* fit 'meadow'); God's gift; Grubbins (cf. Grubbing i, 106 *supra*); Haggdale; Highfield; Hunt deer; Kemp field & paddock; Limekiln close; Mill field (cf. *Milne Inges* 1615, *v.* myln, eng); Notts hill; Pengill; Priest bank; Raise (*v.* hreysi 'cairn'); Reddins (*v.* rydding); Riddlepot; Saturay (a mound, ... *Saterhowe* 1348, *v.* sǽtr haugr); Shepherd Eagle; the Sinkfalls 1731 (ME *sinke* 'conduit, drain,' (ge)fall, 'fall') Slaythornes (cf. *Smaythornes* 1733, probably 'small thorns,' *v.* smár, thorn, but slāh-thorn 'sloe' is also possible); Smiddy acre; Spense; Steel croft (*v.* stigel 'stile'); Stoney park; Stripes (*v.* strīp; 'strip of land'); Tarn tessick (possibly an inversion compound, *v.* tjorn); Whelt (possibly ON hvilft 'hollow' as in Whelter ii, 193 *infra*); Yeat stoops (*v.* geat 'gate,' stólpi).

(*b*)   *Brundehous* (*Broudhous* (sic for *Brond*-) 1302, 'burnt house,' *v.* brende, hūs); *Brownebayne land* 1426 (named from the family of William *Bronbayne* 1292, the name being from ON *brún-beinn* 'brown leg,' cf. the ON bynames *Grábeinn* 'grey leg,' *Hvítbeinn* 'white leg'); *Dupeslaw*; *Edoyneyng* 1426 (possibly an error for the OE fem. pers.n. *Ēadwynn*, *v.* eng); *les Eshpyres* ('ash shoots,' *v.* æsc,spīr); *Kalnestilde* (or *Kalrestyde*) 1292; *Ketelhathes* (ON *Ketill*, *v.* hǽth); Low close 1629; *the Scarthes* 1597 (*v.* skarth 'gap'); *le Storthes* (*v.* storth 'plantation'); *le Tathes* (ON *tatha* 'in-field, manured field,' ...); *Ulmeriddynges* (probably the OE pers.n. *Wulfmēr*, rydding); *Uttyngapefalgh* (*v.* gap 'gap,' falh 'ploughed land,' the first el. may be an OE pers.n. *Utting*, recorded in ME ...); *le Walstorth* (*v.* wall, 'wall, embankment,' storth); *le Waterbankes* (*v.* wæter, banke).

The Place Names of Westmorland includes numerous other old names, of which these are a few examples :

ALAUNA (lost), the name of the Roman fort at Watercrook ... a Brit name.

BOTHELFORD (lost), *Bodelforde* 1086 DB ... 'Ford near the dwelling'... the exact location is unknown, but from its association ... it would appear to be in Natland or Helsington (in the former according to *KCR*); it was probably a ford across the Kent which forms the boundary between these two parishes.

CRACALT HO
Crakehal(e) 1290 ...*Crac-, Crakhal (le)*, 1292, 1312 ...1332 ... *-ell* 1566 ... *et freq* to 1630 ... *Crackhall* 1585 ...
Crakell 1564, 1573 ...
Craycolt 1836 ...
'Nook of land frequented by crows,' *v.* kraka, halh.

WATERCROOK, *Wat(t)ercrook(e)* 1578, 1591 *et freq* to 1627 ... 'Land in the bend of a river,' *v.* waeter, krókr; 'the river [Kent] washes three sides of the ground about it' ... the site of the Roman fort at *Alauna* ...

CASTLESTEADS, 1793 ... 'site of a fort,' *v.* castel, stede, here referring to the remains of an earthwork fort on the Helm ...

CROWPARK, 1777 ... *Crawe(e)parke* 1592 ... 'crow-haunted park,' *v.* cräwe, parke.

NATLAND BECK ... *Nat(t)land Miln(e)beck* 1714 ... 1731 ...
[NATLAND] HALL ... 'the Hall' 1292
      [NATLAND] PARK ... *Nat(e)landpark* 1408 ... 1568

A footnote about the Norsemen in Cumbria: in the *Westmorland Gazette* of September 17th 2004 there was news of the discovery of England's first Viking burial ground, at Cumwhitton, a village near Carlisle. There were shallow graves of two women and four men, along with jewellery, swords, spears, fire-materials and riding equipment. The bodies had been buried in an east-west direction, indicating that they were Christians. These burials probably took place in the early tenth century. There must have been generations of Viking burials in the Natland area: I wonder where!

Chapter 2

1066 AND ALL THAT: A LOOK AT SOME DOCUMENTS

RECORDS OF THE BARONY OF KENDALE

No later invasions modified the Anglian-Scandinavian pattern of settlement in our area. The Norman Conquest of 1066 involved the imposition of a French aristocracy and military class. Natland wasn't mentioned in the Domesday Book of 1086, though strangely, as we have seen, the lost place name 'Bodelforde' does appear. The Norman barons did not venture north-west until 1092, when William Rufus stormed Carlisle, and Cumbria became part of England. Many castles were established to keep order, and many abbeys established at that time. Natland's history becomes clearer, as the village began to appear in documents. The following references are quoted from *Records Relating to the Barony of Kendale*, ed. William Farrer and John F. Curwen, Cumberland and Westmorland Antiquarian and Archaeological Society, 3 vols (Kendal: Titus Wilson, 1923-6), 1, p. 167-175. It is quite remarkable how many of the surnames mentioned in the documents – for example the Walter Strickland's rent roll of 1539, or Thomas Strickland's of 1597 – were to be found in Natland and the surrounding district into the nineteenth and twentieth centuries (Beck, Rowlandson, Mackereth, Sill, Greenbank, Speight, Prickett) and are still to be found in the local telephone directory.

1086 Gilemichel held Bodelforde; *Dom. Bk.* [Domesday Book], f.302.

1170-1180 William de Lancaster … gave to Gervase de Ainecurt, for his homage and service, £15 worth of land yearly, to hold for the service of 3 parts of one knight's fee, namely *inter alia* Natalund and Bothelford [extending] unto the brook of the gallows and so the whole field up to the way from Hoton … to the bounds of Hoton and Stainton.

1190-1200 Gilbert, son of Roger Fitz-Reinfred confirmed to Gervase de Ainecurt the land which William de Lancaster gave to him, namely Natalaund, Bothelford, etc.

1190 Licence granted for mill on the watercourse by the gallows of Kirkeby between Kirkeby and Natalaund. [This was Gallowbarrow, where the unfortunates were buried close to the spot].

1246 Ralph Daincurt gave to master Roger Pepyn, rector of the mediety of the church of Kirkebi in Kendale, land in Natalunt in a competent place, 80 feet in length and 40 in breadth, to hold during his life, for the site of a barn in which to put his tithe of Natalunt.

Roger Pepyn, parson of the mediety of the church of Kyrkeby in Kendale, acknowledged that 14 a [acres] land in Natelund were the right of Ralph de Eyncurt and released them to Ralph for himself and his successors ... and further granted that Ralph and his heirs should henceforth have a chapel in their court at Natelund for the celebration of divine service.

1255-72 Peter de Brus released to William de Stirkeland and Elizabeth his wife their land of Natelund and Syreydberg free from puture of his master forester and all the things belonging to the same forestry [puture being a custom claimed by keepers in forests, and sometimes by bailiffs in Hundreds, to take 'mans-meat,' horse-meat, and dog-meat from the tenants of the forest or thereabouts].

1290 Walter de Stirklaund complains that [several men] came to his land in Nateland and took away his goods and those of Nicholas of Crakehale, his bondman.

1292 Walter, son of Sir William de Strikelande, granted to Robert de Wessington and Joan the grantor's sister ... land in Natelande [held by] William, son of Stephen, ... William Bronbayne, ... Nicholas, son-in-law of Ellen, ... Henry del Grene, ... Richard de Crachalle, ... Richard of the Hall, ... Thomas de Crachalle, ... Nicholas Percy and Henry Glover ... William, the reaper ... Nicholas the shepherd, ... Robert, the miller, ... and Nicholas Parker; ... also the moiety of Lowkerig and the land of John, son of Grete, and the meadow called le Quaghe.

1294 Walter de Styrkelaund impleaded Nicholas de Crakehale, that he render an account of the time he was his bailiff in Nateland.

1302 "Wauter", son of Sir William de Stirklaund, lets to farm to Baudwyn de Schepesheved and Sibyl, his wife, the chief messuage of Natelund with the demesne land and Le Bradynge ... meadow in Staynton, with the wood of Broudhous, which Walter recovered against them by judgment in the King's court, to hold for 9 years from Sunday next before St. Cuthbert in Lent, 30 Edward I, at 45s rent.

1312 An agreement made ... whereby Sir Walter de Stirkland granted to Robert de Wessington and Joan, his wife ... to improve the estate ... in Crakhal, ... in Uttyngapefalgh, ... upon le Bradeflatt, ... near Dupeslaw and on either side of the cross in Nateland, ... and common of pasture in Nateland for themselves and tenants, for all beasts, except goats, outside the hedges at all times, and within the hedges in the town field after the corn and hay have been carried, saving in the lands which Sir Walter holds in severalty and in the wood of Brundehous and le Storthes, and in Loukerigg, which he and Robert and Joan hold in severalty; and liberty to take estovers (except for fuel) in the wastes of Nateland, except in Helm, Alde Nateland, Loukrigg and le Waterbankes, where they shall take rods only; Sir Walter also granted that they should hold the waste, meadow and moss of the Quaghes; all which he granted in exchange for ... le Storthes, ... le Tathes, ... at le Quitestone above the highway, ... between Brundehous and the land of Beatrice la Harpereste and le Walstorth, ... in les Eshspyres and Ulmeriddynges, ... and in Ketelhathes ... , which Sir Walter will presently enclose.

1332	Nateland. Subsidy of a fifteenth.	
	Nicholas the reeve ... in goods ...	30s.
	Robert Routhe ...	15s.
	Richard Warayner ...	45s.
	John son of Agnes ...	30s.
	Nicholas Makerahte ...	15s.
	Robert son of Ellis ...	15s.
	Adam Fisher ...	15s.
	Adam brother of the reeve ...	15s.
	Nelle de Crosthwayt ...	20s.

Sum of goods £10, whereof to the King 13s.4d ...

1348 John, son of Sir Gilbert de Cullewen, kt., granted to Robert, son of Robert de Wessington and his heirs, estovers in his wood of Preston Patrick, necessary for housebote and haybote for Robert's tenants in Nateland.

1377 Adam Bridde impleaded Richard Shephird of Nateland, that he render him 40s. which he has unjustly detained.

1408 Thomas, son and heir of Walter de Stirkeland, chivaler, assigned in dower to dame Alice, late the wife of Sir Walter *inter alia* a park called Natelandpark, a close called Storthepark, in the vill of Helsyngton, a tenement called Ald Nateland, which John Bayley holds at will in the same vill.

1431 Thomas Strykland, knt., pays 34s. for farm of the tithes of Nateland [51 bushels of oatmeal].

1439 Robert Lawrence, knt., held at his death, land and tenements in the vill and hamlet of Nateland, of Thomas de Stirkeland, "chivaler", by service unknown, worth 10 marks yearly; Robert Lawrence his son, aged 40 years, is the next heir.

1494 William, Abbot of St. Mary's, York, and the convent, parsons of the parish church of Kirkeby in Kentdall, let to farm to Thomas Strikeland, kt, for nine years the tithe corn of Nateland for 51s, yearly.

1537 Walter Strykland, upon attaining his majority, had lands and tenements, parcel of the manor of Natland, worth yearly £5 14s.0½d ...

1539 Lease of the tithes of Natland and Whynfell, for 66s. yearly, and for Sysyrehe, 20s., from William, abbot of St. Mary's, York, etc., to William

Knevett, esq., and Lady Katheryn Strykland, his wife.

Rental of Walter Strykland, esq., 1 July, 31 Henry VIII, in Natland with the members: the following took tenements etc. (the sum named being the fine for gressom [a premium paid to a feudal superior on entering upon a holding]).

Roland Becke …	£5
Anthony Langhorne, the tenement late in the tenure of Gervase Rolandson …	£4
Thomas Makerethe, elder …	46s. 8d.
Thomas Makerethe, younger …	£10
John Jaxson …	£3
Thomas Warener …	£5. 6s. 8d.
Henry Grenbanke, ½ tent …	43s. 4d
Nicholas Spyght …	£4
Rowland Saunderson …	£3
William Saunderson …	£6
John Dauber …	£6
William Dauney …	£6
Thomas Spence …	£3
Lawrence Grenbanke, 2 tents …	£3. 10s
Edward Sill, ½ tent …	27s.
Richard Sill, ⅔ tent …	46s. 8d
James Rolondson …	20s.
William Smythe …	40s.
Thomas Syll …	46s. 8d
Christopher Sadelar …	46s. 8d
Richard Bagulay …	40s.
John Lankestre …	40s.
Thomas Cawpland …	33s. 4d
James Cowper took a cottage …	4s. 8d
Edward Sill, the tenement late in the tenure of John Gurnell, and he gave the lord for entry, £4, and for "le tenandright" £12, Sureties: Rowland Becke and Roger Helme.	
Brian Highyn, a cottage …	10s.
Milles Cowper, a tent.4 marks, Sureties; Edward Sill, and Peter Chamer.	
William Scheppard, a cottage …	10s.
Hengon Hudson, a cottage …	10s.

1540 "The booke off Walter Strykelande, esquyer. etc., of his tenandes and inhabitants" within Natland: *each with horse, harnes and a bowe*, Thomas Macareth, elder, Lawrance Grenebanke, James Rowlandson, Mylles

Robynson, Roger Pryket, Mylles Kowper, James Pryket, Christoper Bek.

Bylmen, with horse, harnes and a byll: Thomas Waryner, Thomas Syll, Wylliam Sanderson, William Smythe, Edward (*cancelled*) Thomas Macarethe, Thomas (*cancelled*) John Wylliamson, John (*cancelled*), Edward Benson, William Strykeland, James Robynson, Robert Pryket, Robert Makareth, Martyn Gylpyn.

Foytmen with sum harnes, oder none: Thomas Spence, a jak, a sallet, and a bow; Rowlland Pryket, harnese and a bow; Hew Hodson, a bow, Bryan Hyggyn, a bow.

Bylles: John Atkynson, a jake and a byll; Mycall Spyght, a sallet and a byll; Robert Strykland, the same; Henry Grenebanke, James Kowper, Edward Syll, William Schipert [each] a byll; Edward Sill "h.h. a bowe".

Yongmen bowys (each had a bow): Nycholes Scherman, Wylliam Scherman, Roger Walker, John Nykson, Robert Waryner (*these 5 cancelled*), Wylliam Jhonson, John Cowper (*cancelled*).

Bylles (each had a bill: James Toorner. George Bowman, Lawrance Sanderson, Leonard Cowper (*cancelled*), Peter Cowper, Robert Macareth (*cancelled*) Jhon Barray, Nycholes Macareth, Brian Denneson, Hene Nycolson, John Ingerson, Wylliam Shepert, James Walker, Tomas Cowpland, John Lancaster.

[These were obliged to turn out in the event of any civil disturbance: in other words, they were the Lord of the Manor's 'Dads' Army.']

1569 After the death of Walter Strickland, the Court of Wards granted to Alice his relict ... the manor of Natland ... messuages and lands in Crakell ... a pasture in Lawkrigge ... the manor of Whinfell ... a tenement in Sleadall ... a tenement in Staveley ... out of which rents the said Alice took one third for dower and paid about two-thirds as rent to the Court of Wards.

1585 Manors, lands, etc., of Thomas Strycklande, which descended to him after the death of Walter, his father ... The manor of Natland, held of the heirs of Thomas Parre, knt., as of the 4th part of the barony of Kendall by knight's service ... 2 messuages in Crackhall, ... 15 a.[acres] in Lawkrigge, ... a pasture of 16 a. and 30 a. wood called Natland Park.

1588 William Langhorne of Natland, yeoman, assigns to Thomas Langhorne, his brother, of Kingston upon Thames, tailor, a tenement in Natland, late in the occupation of Anthony Langhorne, deceased, and now of the said William ...

1597 Thomas Strickland's rent roll in Natland, made 1 August, 39 Elizabeth, 1597.

Edward Cowper
John Syll
Walter Grenebanck
Edmond Grenebanck
Anthony Spence
Lawrence Williamson
Relict of Robert Willson
Christopher Newby
Edward Dawney
Edward Mackereth
Thomas Makereth
Brian Dickson
Robert Strickland, for the tenement, late in the holding of
Edmund his father, gressom £5, hauling silver and 9s.10p.
Relict of John Mackereth
Peter Williamson

James Speyht
William Sleddall
Nicholas Warryner
Henry Robinson
Hugh Jackson
Relict of Jas. Rollandson
Jas. Rollandson for a close
Alan Prickett
Barnard Crosbye
William Prickett
William Shepard, 3s. 4d.
William Strickland

Lawrence Williamson
Brian Shawe

Lawrence Williamson and Peter Shepard, 23s. 4d. Peter Shepherd
(for his fine of half that tenement which his father and he jointly
held, being tenant of the other moiety before, rent 5s., gressome,
40s. and for fine of a cottage rent, 3s. 4d., gressome, 10s.) and
William Sheperd, 1 hen for hauling silver and 9s. 1½ d. Relict of
William Sheppard (for her heriot of half the Scarthes, 40s.) 23s. 4d.

Richard Robinson
Robert Robinson
Thomas Haulehed
Miles Robinson
Thomas Haulehed

Robert Prickett
William Prickett
Cuthbert Fisher
The relict of Edward Sill
Robert Beck

['Hallage' was an obligation connected with the use of a hall, 'heriot' a
payment due to the lord of a fee on the death of a tenant]

1670 – A Breviat of all the hearths chargeable.
32 in number – £1 12 0 tax.

Mr William Grey …	4	Nich: Hollowhead …	1
Mr John Wilkinson	2	Chr: Prickett …	2
Math: Range …	1	Tho: Kitchine …	1
Tho: Lickbarrow …	2	Rich: Robinson …	1
Tho: Sheapherd …	2	Mr John Hadwen …	2
Willm Robinson …	1	Tho: Wilson …	2
Edmond Strickland	1	Willm Wilson …	1
James Jackson …	2	Rich: Robinson …	1
Walter Cowper …	1	These persons following are	
John Atkinson …	1	discharged by Certificates.	
Robt. Lea	1	Robt. Hodghson …	1
John Powe …	2	Widdow Kitchin …	1
James Garnett …	1		

MORE RECORDS: ROADS AND BRIDGES

In his Introduction to the third volume of *Records Relating to the Barony of Kendale*, John F. Curwen gives us a useful account of the course of the main road north, based on John Ogilby's survey of the principal roads of England, undertaken with the authority of Parliament and completed by 1675. North of Heron Syke, we are told, the road 'passes through Burton, along the western boundary of "Holmes Park," "Frandon,"over the Peasy Beck near "Preston Chapel," over "Sallat Brow," to the west of "Grove Chappell" *i.e.* the old Crosscrake Chapel, through "Notclaf" and over "Neither Bridg" to Kendal at 256 miles from London.' (*Records*, 3, p. 5). 'Notclaf,' improbably enough, is Ogilby's version of Natland. The main road evidently followed the present-day lane from Crosscrake to Newlands, going through Natland and into Kendal along the present road.

Records Relating to the Barony of Kendale also contains references, most of them from the Indictment and Order Books, to the state of repair of roads and bridges in and around Natland. These are a few examples from the late seventeenth and early eighteenth centuries (*Records*, 3, pp. 112-13):

1671 6 October. The highway from Sedgwick to K. Kendall from Middle Lawkrigg in Natland to land adjoining Watercrook, is in great decay and ought to be repaired by the inhabitants of Natland.

1679 10 October. Order for the repair of a foot bridge called Natland Bridge which is fallen down and not passable.

1692 15 January Presentment that Hawes Bridge is in decay; Order for an estimate of the charge of repair.

1705/6 18 January Order the high constables to view Hawes Bridge over the River Kent, it being a public bridge, and to speedily contract with workmen for the effectual repair thereof.

1710 21 April. Presentment that the public bridge, called Hawes Bridge, is out of repair, the ledges on both sides being broken down, by the late flood, for the length of 8 or 9 yards. Order to the high constables to view and repair the same.

1710 6 October. Presentment by John Archer, esqr., that the highway from Pottbeck to Oxen Holme is very ruinous; order for repair before 1 December, by the inhabitants under pain of £10 fine.

1720 7 October. Presentment that the highway from Great Shedlings [Gate Settlings] to Hellern [Helm] End and thence to Barwis Green is in great decay.

1730/1 15 January. ...Benjamin Brown reported that the way from Natland Milnbeck to the Sinkfalls is the most part of it very narrow and the wood covers it very much, especially thorn and hazel; and the way from the said Milnbeck to Natland and from thence to Sedgwick is likewise very narrow and much covered with thorn and hazel.

John Leland's Itinerary

John Leland (1506?-1552) was appointed King's Antiquary by Henry VIII in 1533. He toured England and Wales, describing buildings and collections of antiquarian interest, including monasteries and their libraries – no doubt partly in order to ascertain what riches Henry could acquire. In his Itinerary, compiled between 1535 and 1543, he describes his journey through Lancashire and north of Lancaster into Westmorland. He had obviously ridden through Natland, noting that it was good farming country:

> By Bitham is a great parke and a goodly place yn hit of the Erle of Darby. By Bytham rennith Byth water a preaty river, and by likelihod shuld resort toward Kennet.

> Thens I roode over a great bek caullid Staunton Bekke, and so ridding a ii. miles farther cam to a soile lesse stony and more fruteful of corne, as sum whete, much ootes and barle, or bigge, and so to Kendale riding over Ken river. Ther be about Kendale divers fair woddes, as Master Parris parke, and many other. Kendale is countid as baronry, wherof Mr Par is possessor.

(*The Itinerary of John Leland In or About the Years 1535-1543*, ed. Lucy Toulmin Smith, 5 vols [London: George Bell & Sons, 1907-1910], 4, p.12)

Order Books and Indictment Books

Many Natland people faced terrible poverty and other hardships, some of which are reflected in official documents kept in the Kendal Archives. Here are a few examples, quoted, and in some cases summarised, from Order Books and Indictment Books (in several places the handwriting is illegible):

1696 – Petition of Richard Bulfield of Natland showing that he had served as constable of Natland forthwith for many years but by reason of his great age and infirmity he is not able to serve any longer. It is therefore ordered that the next in turn shall execute the said office and take on him the office of constable aforesaid within a week.

1698 – Humble petition of Richard Bullfoll of Natland showing that he hath been hired as constable for Natland for some time and that his wages … being very poor is not able to support himself and small children … ordered that the award be paid … for the times he has served as constable by those in turn and further to be relieved according to his … [partly illegible].

1698 – The Surveyors of the Highways for Natland have not their highways in good repair to the great disturbance of the passengers that have occasion to … that it being the King's highway. It is ordered that the said surveyors have their ways in good orderly repair within the space of one month … surveyors to forfeit … shillings.

1700 – Whereas it appears to the court upon the oath of Thomas Towers that he had lived at Natland for seven years, is respected and has maintained himself and family hitherto without being chargeable to the hamlet and now being reduced to poverty is at a want of a house to live in. It is therefore ordered that the inhabitants of Natland find him a house to live in.

1704 – Paid to John King of Natland … for his repair of the county bridge Haws Bridge … 00.03.06.

1727 – Judith Newton single woman of Natland had bastard child by George Squire … but … Robert Shipherd of Natland … John Anderson of Natland … putative father of her child had absconded … [indecipherable – but possibly the parish had to pay for upkeep of child].

1728 [at Christmas] Appeal made by Churchwardens and Overseers of the poor of Natland – against removal of John Dixon and family from Barbon to Natland. Legal settlement made absolute.

1729 – Petition of Thomas Postlethwaite of Natland showing that he has infirm wife and two small children – by reason hearby notwithstanding his … to support them is not without … Pay T. Postlethwaite the sum of 9d weekly and 2/6d for the charge of this order.

1729 – Petition of Thomas Postlethwaite of Natland, showing that Rachel his wife and two small children are very poor and must inevitably starve without the charity of the hamlet, having an allowance of 9d a week formerly – granted towards their relief and maintenance, it is therefore ordered that the sum of 9d a week be from henceforth continued to be payed [sic] by the Churchwardens and Overseers of Natland aforesaid till further order.

1734 [in a Minute Book] – Petitions of Daniel Dobson of Natland for resumption of relief paid to him till now by township for maintaining bastard child – referred to D. Archer.
Recognizances of – John Anderton his wife Margaret, Robert Kemp, husbandman, and Edward Shepherd gent, all of Natland, for appearance of Margaret and good behaviour to Agnes Postlethwaite 1 Aug.1734 – discharged.

1735-6 [at Christmas] – Writ to summon inhabitants of Natland and Stainton for neglecting highway from Sinkfall Gate to Richard Dickinson's house and thence to Roger Dickinson's house – appeared and discharged.

1737 – John Airey (or Varey) and family removed from Kirkland to Natland

– they had been legally settled at Natland in 1728. [This includes a long homily about the illicit relations of this John Airey's father].

1739 – Warrant for removal of John Bulfield wife and daughter from Natland to Stainton, but their last legal settlement was at Natland - warrant made void.

1739 – Inhabitants of Natland had been ordered to pay 2/- a week towards maintenance of Rebecca Thompson and pay house rent which they thought excessive; instead they were ordered to pay 1/6 plus house rent.

1739 [at Christmas] Warrant for removal of John Bulfield wife and daughter from Natland to Stainton, but their last legal settlement was at Natland, warrant made void.

1748 [at Christmas] – Distemper of cattle – all markets for sale of cattle within Kendal and Lunesdale Wards prohibited till further order.

1784 – Hawes Bridge – one of the public bridges belonging to the County of Westmorland. Bridge and 300 ft of road at each end in great decay – to be repaired at expense of County.

1801 [at Christmas] Allowance for conveying migrants –
        On foot 2d per mile.
        On horseback 4d per mile.
        By cart 5d.
        For every meal 4d.

1812 – John Petty, attorney at law, Kirkland, to keep the peace especially towards William Bateman.

1816 – In this session likewise filed the several convictions of John Atkinson, husbandman, Josias Herd Harling of Levens, mariner, and Richard Smith of Kirkby Kendal, labourer, in the penalty of £10 each for using guns for the purpose of taking and killing game.
[Also under 1816 there is an interesting reference to a flax-dresser in Kirkland].

1820 – James Briggs of Natland Mill Beck, engineer, to appear and prefer a Bill of Indictment against Robert Rennison of Kby Kendal, for feloniously stealing, taking away one wheelbarrow of the value of sixpence of the goods and chattels of the Company of Proprietors of the Lancaster Canal Navigation. Sent to the House of Correction for one week.

1825 – ... also is filed the Consent of the Proprietors of the Lancaster Canal Navigation, owners of the land mentioned in the said plan to the making and continuing of the new roads respectively mentioned offer.

1832 – Natland assigned to Kendal for polling.

1845 – [About this time 'Lunatics and Idiots' of Westmorland were confined to an asylum, Dunston Lodge near Newcastle-on Tyne: fifteen were sent from Westmorland, 'tho Cumberland had been sending them there before Westmorland.']

1852 – Constables to be – Milnthorpe, Ambleside, Kendal (including Natland) – at 17/- per week plus 1 suit of uniform annually, coat, 2 prs trousers, 2 prs boots, one hat & stock and a cape – and a greatcoat once every 2 years.

1866 – [References to Cattle Plague: by 1870 this is sometimes referred to as Foot and Mouth disease].

1876 – [Cattle plague was still rife: the Chief Constable was authorised in every case of suspicion of that disease to call in a Veterinary Surgeon and under his advice must order the immediate slaughter of any animal affected. Without further instruction, in case of appearance of plague in the County – the Chief Constable to appoint a sufficient number of additional constables to form a cordon round the infected place etc., etc. He must ensure full inspection of fairs, markets, on the Beast Banks and the Auction Mart].

From the Indictment Book:

1846	Thomas Creighton of Natland, fined 5s....drunk.		
	William Carradice	”	” ” ”
	Edward Warriner	”	in penalty £2 for selling game without licence.
	Johnathan Just	”	in sum of 6d &n £1/ 4/ 6 costs beating one James Sim.
	William Carradice	”	penalty £1 for fighting.
1849 –	Thomas Crieghton	”	fined 5s. drunk.
1850 –			
	Johnathan Just	”	7s and costs for assaulting John Mitchell.
	William Carradice	”	5s....drunk.
	Richard Troughton		10s & costs for assaulting Thomas Carradice.

PARISH REGISTERS OF KENDAL

The late sixteenth and early seventeenth centuries were times of real deprivation. Sheer starvation weakened the people, especially the poor, who frequently succumbed to 'the diseases of the people' – plague, tuberculosis, cholera, dysentery, smallpox and leprosy. Poor hygienic arrangements and lack of a safe water supply contributed to the spread of disease. We know that Kendal was ravaged by the plague: some of the deaths recorded there might have included poor people who had come in from the countryside seeking charity. For details of Natland folk we have to consult the Parish Registers of Births, Marriages and Deaths of Kendal: it was only in 1777 that Natland started to keep its own registers. Here are a few examples of christenings:

1558 – July 21	– Robert, s. of Rowland Makereth of Natland.	
Oct 22	– Margrett, d. of Thomas Robinson of	"
1559 – Jan 31	– Isabell, d. of Rowland Makereth of	"
Apr 7	– Robert, s. of Robert Makereth of	"
Sept 21	– Thomas, s. of Thomas Prickett of	"
" 23	– Robert, s. of William Shepherd of	"

Babies born out of wedlock are mentioned quite frequently, as for example:

1572 – May 10 – Maryan. Ye supposed daughter of Thomas
Robinson

There are a number of references to 'bastards:' 'illegitimate' would have been a slightly kinder description. Oddly there was a preponderance of boys in this group, and they were often given the Christian name of the supposed father. Of the girls, many were christened Agnes. There were several christenings of children of strangers and travellers. At this time the place of birth is seldom given. When the father is of higher status than normal, he is given the title 'Mr.'

Among the marriages recorded in the Parish Registers are the following:

1557 – Feb 11	– Thomas Prickett, Margrett Robinson	"
1558 – Oct 24	– John Mackreth, Agnes Prickett	"
1559 – Jan 30	– John Goffe, Jennet Prickett	"
" – Jul 10	– Edmund Greenebanke, Anne Becke	"
1561 – Jul 14	– Roger Cowper, Isabell Cresta (Chester)	"

[From 1570 no place of residence is given, so we may be missing some Natland marriages up to 1575].

1576 – Jul 16	– Edmund Strickland, Agnes Brathwaite	"
" " 28	– William Mackereth, Isabell Gilpin	"

And finally burials:

1594 – Mar 25	– William s. of Anthony Turner, of Natland	
" – Apr 3	– Alice, d, of John Turner	"
" " 4	– Thomas Mackrethe	"
" " 23	– Janet, 1. w. [?] of Thomas Macarath	"
" – July 1	– Ellin, d. of Edmund Strickland	"
" – Aug 15	– Thomas, s. of Robert Prickett	"
" " 24	– Maryon, d. of Oswald Speight	"
" – Sep 2	– James, s. of Anthony Turner	"
" " 23	– Margrett, d. of James Rowlandson	"
" – Dec 3	– Edward, s. of James Rowlandson	"

There are references to the burials of several still-born babies, and to those of babies with no Christian name given ('a sone of'). Sometimes the reference to the place of birth is very specific, e.g. Cracalt or Watercrook.

FIELD ENCLOSURES

The date of field enclosures in Natland is impossible to ascertain, though some field names are recorded as early as 1292. Several of the early field names, as we have seen, have a distinctly Norse flavour. One, 'le Tathes,' is Old Norse for in-field or manured field; in the case of 'Uttyngapefalgh,' 'Utting' may be an Anglian personal name, while 'falgh' is ploughed land, probably referring to open-field cultivation. Perhaps some of the enclosures were made about the time (1694) when the Stricklands sold their properties in Natland to their tenants, retaining only their manorial rights, which the family still holds today. The local six inches to a mile (1:10,560) Ordnance Survey map, sheet SD 58 NW, shows clearly the fields on the east side of the village behind Long Meadow Lane, with parallel walls running uphill, probably marking the borders of the groups of field strips, or 'dales' as they are sometimes known; there are also cross walls. These parallel walls can be traced all round the village on the map, rather indistinct in places where fields have been joined together. The field pattern resembles a spider's web. In a few places, given a certain light, or a day of frost or a light snowfall, one can pick out the ridge and furrow pattern of the old ploughing.

The fact of working together in open-field culture must have resulted in a close community. The feudal tenants worked a system of rotation of crops, including a period of fallow; their grain crops were mainly oats and barley, both able to thrive in these northern parts. They had to cooperate in such matters as access to individual strips, times of ploughing, sowing, harrowing and harvesting, pasturing of cattle on the stubble of harvested fields and on the fallow. Sown fields had to be protected from trespass by cattle or intruders. Field enclosures doubtless gave a stimulus to the farmers to improve their stock, and this process has continued right up to the present day: the farmers of two or three centuries ago would hardly recognise the farm animals of today.

HELM: NATLAND'S COMMON

Natland still has its common land, Helm, which belongs to the Lord of the Manor at Sizergh Castle. Its boundary wall runs along the top of the hill, bounded there by Stainton's one-time common, which was sold years ago. We are lucky to retain our side of the hill as common land. At one time Helm was used by villagers for grazing their cattle. The common is still managed by the Commoners, who nowadays let their rights to a single tenant. We hope we can keep our 'right to roam,' the free access that dates back beyond the memory of anyone alive today. In a newspaper article of 1987, we were told: 'No fencing can take place on any common without, in England, the consent of the Secretary of State for the Environment. The owner is not allowed to do anything that interferes with the rights of the commoners. So he cannot afforest the land or build houses on it.' These rules have helped to ensure that commons remain as open tracts of land: let us hope that they continue to be observed.

Kendal Corn Rent Map: Owners and Tenants

The manuscript schedule for the Kendal Corn Rent map of 1836 tells us much about the field pattern and field use at this time. The fields are numbered, but not in numerical order. Names of owners are indicated by capitals, while those of tenants appear in lower-case:

MR BULLFIELD
No. 3, Sarah Bullfield, cottage, barn and garden
    38, himself, public house and orchard (later Horse & Farrier Inn)

A full list together with map is in the Appendix.

Natland Park

Most villages sported a park of one kind or another, usually owned by the Lord of the Manor, with severe penalties imposed for poaching. In 1585 'a pasture of 16 a. [acres] and 30 a. wood called Natland Park, worth yearly, 16s. 8d' were listed among the 'Manors, lands, etc.' of Thomas 'Strycklande.' When the Rev. Machell visited Natland in 1691, he recorded the park as having been disparked long since. Still remaining were about 80 acres 'walled six quarters high' ('six quarters' is 4 feet 6 inches, a 'quarter' being 9 inches). The walls must have been very substantial. In 1968 the Kendal road was widened, and much of the remaining portion of the old park wall was destroyed. A short section of the old wall forms part of a garden wall on the left hand side of Oxenholme Lane, up past the School. Some stones from the park wall would doubtless be used for building the walls within the former park, and some for local building; some, we know, were used as ballast on the canal barges, and taken to Preston for paving the streets.

Three cottages called Park Cottages lie on the corner, across the road from Natland Hall. I can't trace their origin, but at one time they were owned by the Wakefield family: no doubt they housed some of the employees at the Wakefields' Gunpowder Works at Sedgwick. A number of alterations have been made over the years. The length of old cobbled paving in front of the cottages, which was always in public use, has in recent years been edged with white-painted stones, forcing pedestrians, including children and old

The Pound

Courtesy late Mrs. Maples

people, to walk on the road itself – close to an extremely dangerous corner. Across the road from the cottages there was a very old enclosure called the Pound, or Pinfold: it was here that stray animals were kept safely until claimed by the owner. There must have been some arrangement for feeding and watering. Years ago Mr Billy Kitchin used to keep hens there. The Pound disappeared during the road widening of 1968.

Early picture of Natland PO. On the left is Natland Hall farm building and the 'Pound' can just be seen between the farm building and Park Cottages.

Courtesy Graham Needham

Natland Mill Beck with old mill behind.
Courtesy Local Studies Section, Kendal Library

NATLAND MILL

The history of Natland Mill goes back many centuries. In 1170-80 'William de Lancastre II. gave to Gervase de Ainecurt, for his homage and service, £15 worth of land yearly to hold for the service of 3 parts of one knight's fee, namely *inter alia* Natalund and Bothelford [extending] unto the brook of the gallows and so the whole field up to the way from Hoton …to the bounds of Hoton and Stainton' (see above, 'Records of the Barony of Kendale'). The hill on the Kendal side of Natland Beck, formerly a rubbish tip and now built up with houses, is still called Gallowbarrow – the site of the Kendal gallows; the unfortunate criminals were doubtless buried close by. A document of 1190-1200 records that 'Gilbert son of Roger Fitz-Reinfred confirms to Gervase de Ainecurt the land which William de Lancastre father of Helewise, the grantor's wife, gave to him, namely Natalaund, Bothelford, … with licence to make a mill on the water course by the gallows of Kirkeby between Kirkeby and Natalaund' (*Records*, 1, p. 131). In 1292 Robert was the miller (see above, 'Records of the Barony of Kendale'), and a document of 1526 refers to 'Thomas Syll of Natlandmyln' (*Records*, 2, p. 195), perhaps the same Thomas Syll mentioned in documents of 1539 and *c.* 1540. Jordans of Kendal owned the mill latterly, and it was last worked for grain in 1935; for four years it was used to generate electricity for Helme Lodge. It seemed a sad end to such a long and useful life.

The streams supplying power to Natland Mill had their sources in Spindle Woods and Kendal Parks, and a large mill pond lay between the Burton and Oxenholme roads. During one flood a herd of pigs was seen to swim to safety across the swollen beck.

Chapter 3

TOWARDS MODERN TIMES

FARMING: LIVING AND WORKING CONDITIONS IN THE NINETEENTH CENTURY

Frank W. Garnett's *Westmorland Agriculture 1800-1900* (Kendal: Titus Wilson, 1912) is a fascinating account of traditional farming life in our area (the name Garnett, incidentally, crops up in Natland again and again). In the following sections I quote largely from my notes on Mr Garnett's book.

Before the seventeenth century most smaller dwellings were built round a 'cruck' frame – that is, two or three pairs of curved, roughly worked timbers (siles), set on low drystone walls, and pegged at the apex to form an 'A' shape. The low walls were then raised in height, the gable ends built, and the steeply pitched roof thatched or slated. Later the houses of 'statesmen' and farmers were built of rough-hewn stone with slate roof where obtainable, or else heather or rush thatch. The price of roofing slate in Kendal in 1786, per rood of $42\frac{1}{4}$ square yards, was £1 3s 4d for the coarsest, and £1 15s for the finest. (I think the Natland houses would have slate roofs.) There were usually a few trees round the house, and often a cheese press against one of the trees, and a small garden for potherbs and bees. The door of the sanitary arrangements often opened directly onto the

Miss Lily Hutchinson, with Molly, delivering milk on Helmside Road, Oxenholme in 1889.
Courtesy late Mrs. Maples

'middenstead.' The kitchen was the principal room, with slate flags or cobbled floor, or beaten earth. There would be a large funnel-shaped fireplace with settles (long high-backed seats) on either side of the 'rannel-balk,' and on the sides of the chimney were hung beef, mutton and bacon to be smoked for keeping purposes. Peats and wood would be burnt. Men and women both sat there on winter nights, carding wool, spinning, and knitting stockings; to ensure good wear the stocking heels were often smeared with melted pitch. Children 'teased' and cleaned wool. No time was wasted and knitting was done in odd moments of the day. A passage called the 'hallen' separated the kitchen from the bower, where the master and mistress slept, and from the 'mell' or dairy. Opposite the latter and behind the kitchen was the 'down-house,' a single storied building where the 'fire-elding' (fire wood) was kept, and where brewing and baking were often done. Servants and children slept above the kitchen and bower, in the unceiled loft, the sexes being divided by only a curtain, (by the end of the nineteenth century these matters improved). This loft was often approached by stone steps outside the back door.

Wooden trenchers served for plates, small wood vessels called 'piggins' for liquids and 'hasty' (porridge). Pewter vessels were used in richer statesmen's houses; later earthenware was used everywhere. Candles were made from mutton or bacon fat, with wicks of the pith of rushes – these were used in rough iron sconces stuck into a heavy wooden block, which could be raised or lowered by a ratchet. For baking unleavened bread a griddle was used – a 26-inch-diameter iron disk placed upon a three-legged iron brandreth, which was 8 inches high and 13 wide at the rim; this was placed over the open hearth fire. 'Haver' (oatmeal) bread, otherwise known as 'clapbread,' was made on it, baked in quantity to last a month or so. It was stored in a large oak chest, usually rudely carved with the family's initials and date when made. The chest stood opposite the fire to keep the contents dry.

What little coal was used was brought from Ingleton on the backs of Galloway ponies, or from the port at Milnthorpe. Peat fires were kept burning, often for generations, kindled with difficulty – if allowed to go out – with flint, steel and a tinder box containing charred linen rags and home-made strips of wood dipped in sulphur.

Food was the product of the grain they grew, oats and barley, with a few potatoes (in later years), and meat that was killed in the autumn. The grain was crushed at the nearest mill. Wheaten bread was only for special occasions such as christenings and funerals. At funerals small loaves called 'arvel' bread were given to invited guests, who took them home and ate them in remembrance of their deceased neighbour. This custom survived as late as 1834. Sometimes the bread was made with sour leaven or yeast. Barley mixed with rye made good bread, and was used in poorer homes about 1840. Eventually wheaten bread was used generally, except in the poorest homes. Brown bread was common, made with a mixture of wheat and barley, or wheat. 'Hasty' pudding was thick porridge made from oatmeal and water, eaten with butter, milk, treacle, beer or cheese, and usually constituted the principal part of both morning and evening meals. At the midday meal meat was eaten whilst the store lasted. A piece boiled on Sunday was then used cold on following days. Soup flavoured with pot herbs could also be poured over meal, and this was called 'crowdy.' Blue-milk cheese, called 'wangy,' and beer, were always on the table. Masters and servants ate together. On larger farms barley was made into malt, using a malt-mill, like a big coffee grinder.

Meat killed about Martinmas could be pickled in large pickling tubs, dried, or smoked in the chimney for preservation. Few animals were killed after Christmas till the following summer, with the exception of bull calves, which were sent to market at two to three weeks and killed for veal. Pigs were slaughtered between Christmas and Candlemas (2nd February). A butcher or grazier might supply a customer with a quarter or side of beef that was dried in the chimney for summer use, or put in brine for winter. They could also have dried mutton legs, or salmon. They had a custom of making pies of minced mutton, fruit and sugar at Christmas time, so-called 'sweet pie' (I had some of this at a Christmas party a very long time ago, and it was not to my taste at all). Bull beef was not allowed to be sold unless it had been 'baited,' under penalty of a fine of 3s 4d (baiting by dogs was believed to improve the flavour). This practice was discontinued in Kendal (on Beast Banks) in 1791, in Appleby in 1820, and in Kirkby Stephen in 1824.

As to clothes – the rough grey wool of native sheep was carded and spun at home. It was woven into cloth by the nearest village weaver, and this cloth was called self-grey or duffel, and was sometimes dyed blue. Blue was the favourite colour for worsted stockings. Men generally wore knee breeches; some wore buckskin ones for special occasions. Itinerant tailors made up 'duffel' or 'hodden-grey' for men, and finer stuff called 'russet' for the womenfolk. Wages for the tailor were 10d to 1s per day, plus food and lodging; they stayed till the family's and servants' clothes were complete. Clothes formed a considerable part of the wages of female servants. Pedlars of small items also acted as newsmen, newspapers being too dear. There was a custom, in some outlying districts, for at least one farmer to attend church and carry back the week's news to the rest of the dale. In the church porch were the dates of sales and fairs, of notices of strayed and lost sheep, and all matters of public interest – or these might be announced from a tombstone after the service. Labouring people wore clogs with soles of alder wood: these were widely worn on farms both inside and out.

The farm barns were of sufficient size to accommodate the whole hay and farm produce: outside haystacks were rare in this area. Shippons and stables were low and without light or ventilation. Floors were of beaten earth or paved with cobbles. Little or no bedding was used for horses and none for cattle. Ash bands – pliable young branches – were used for tethering animals. There were few farm implements and those were simple and homemade. A light wooden 'swing-plough' was drawn by two or three horses. Winnowing machines became fairly common on larger farms – previously a windy day was needed to blow the chaff from the corn on the nearest elevation – a 'deeting' hill. Many barns had a small door opposite a larger entrance, to create the necessary draught to winnow the grain as it was poured over the edge of a 'weyt,' a kind of shallow dish made of a sheepskin fixed over a hoop.

There were variations of tenure. Many small farms were occupied by land held under the lord of the manor chiefly by customary tenure or in freehold, similar to copyhold. The occupiers were known as 'statesmen,' with small holdings with a value of £10-20, occasionally up to £50 a year; a few paid £200-250 a year in rent. Statesmen constituted a peasant proprietary, which at one time occupied nearly the whole of the county. Where the holding was small the common rights helped to ensure the maintenance of a family in fair comfort; in fact they might be able to educate a younger son for the Church etc. The statesmen were sincere and honest, tenacious of old established customs, laborious and content with plain and wholesome food. Injustice and fraud were almost unknown.

The enclosed lands were bounded by hedges and walls. In early winter ash trees in hedges and along roads were lopped, and the branches strewn in the fields for sheep and cattle to browse. Farmers also had the common for extra grazing, and there was an unwritten law that no one should send more stock to the common than they could winter at home. Later, in 1907, an Act of Parliament prohibited the pasturing on the commons of entire (uncastrated) male animals. These had to be kept in the enclosed fields, enabling the farmers to improve the breeds of their stock. The ewes were kept as long as they could breed – ten to fifteen years if they lived that long – then sold for about 6s a head. Six fleeces weighed a stone and sold at about 5d per pound. Cattle were as backward as the sheep, mostly the black Galloway type, crossed with the Longhorn type or Irish Killoes. Young cattle were never housed, and there was little fattening of them in winter.

The quantity of land under the plough was barely sufficient to produce the oats and barley required by the farmer and his family, as grass had priority to feed cattle and sheep. Oats were brought in: there were markets for oats at Penrith and Burton until the Kendal to Lancaster Canal was opened in 1819, when the main market was transferred to Kendal. The system of crop rotation was practised, and some other crops were grown – potatoes, clovers, etc. There was a custom in this area whereby the farmer ploughed and manured a field and then let parcels of it to local labourers who planted potatoes and took all risk of the crop at 2s per perch or 'foe.' By 1812 the price had risen to 3s 9d and 4s 9d.

Butter was made in summer, salted and put in firkins (wooden tubs), weighing 56 pounds and sold at market to dealers from Lancashire and Yorkshire, at 30s to 35s each firkin. New milk was sold at 1d per quart: in Kendal it brought $1\frac{1}{2}$d per quart, and skimmed milk $\frac{1}{2}$d per quart. A cow in milk would be worth £10, and would cost about 7s 6d to keep on the common from May to October. Three year-old barren heifers would be worth £5 to £8 each, heifers in calf £7. 10s to £10 each. Wages for male servants, with victuals, were paid £6 to £10 a year; and maidservants £3 to £4, common labourers, 12d in summer, 8d in winter, per day – with victuals. Men hired by the month for haytime and harvest received £2 to £3, women 16s to £1. 7s, boys 12s to £1. 4s, all with victuals and drink. After the harvest they could earn 5s to 6s a week with knitting.

Most of the farm labourers of Westmorland were unmarried men who had board and lodging at the farm. In the early years of the nineteenth century they were hired at Whitsuntide for the year, but later, with the introduction of hirings at Martinmas, hiring could be for the half year. From about 1829 women could be hired here too. Those to be hired wore some token, such as a straw or a flower in one's cap. Bargaining for wages was sealed by a shilling given to the servant – 'yearl' or 'arl' money. Farm servants had a week's holiday at the end of each term. Some were hired at Kendal's Spring Cattle Fair, which was a general servant's holiday at that time. There was a fair, races, wrestling, cock-fighting, children's processions, singing, dancing and someone played a fiddle: in fact it was a time of merry-making, a welcome change from the servants' hard working lives. Some farmers kept their children off school at haytime and other busy times.

On the farm the old up-and-down churn was commonly used. Cream was kept for long periods in small dairies and carefully stirred with a rowan stick, supposedly to prevent it being 'witched' or spoiled by the host of evil spirits that lurked everywhere. The rowan, or mountain ash, guaranteed protection, having magical properties. A milk separator was introduced in 1895: this separated the cream from the milk, and made butter making easier. The average yield of milk was then only 570 gallons from each cow per annum, and it took 3 gallons of milk to produce 1 pound of butter. Little cheese was made, mostly blue-milk cheese, and it was eaten on the farm. There were three main breeds of sheep – Black-Faced Heath, Herdwicks and Silverdales. During the nineteenth century the Black-Faced breed was improved and developed to three distinct varieties – Scotch, Rough Fell and

Swaledale. Garnett notes that some Herdwicks had a singular anatomical character, having one rib more than any other breed, fourteen instead of thirteeen! Herdwicks, incidentally, take their name from a mode of agriculture peculiar to the area where they were most commonly farmed, the Lake District. The farms on which they were pastured were called 'herdwicks,' and sheep and lands were let together, the flock belonging to the land. Formerly sheep were salved with a mixture of butter and tar, a custom that continued elsewhere; but 'dipping' started about 1840. In 1905 the Board of Agriculture issued a compulsory dipping order, and from 1912 sheep had to be dipped twice a year. Dipping prevented fly infestation, especially in warm weather.

In South Westmorland, Longhorn and Galloway cattle were the usual breeds. In 1794 the expense of keeping a cow was about £5 a year, and produced about £8. The last record of a pure-bred Longhorn was at Shap Fair in 1885. Shorthorn cattle were introduced about 1810 and were popular by 1812. Mr Simm, farming at Watercrook about 1827, was one of the earliest Shorthorn breeders in this district. By 1888 Ed Mason, then farming Watercrook, was among the chief Shorthorn breeders. The cattle wealth of the county lay in the non-pedigree Shorthorns.

The hardy fell Galloway ponies persisted for a long time, and still run semi-wild and breed on the fells. The big strong Clydesdale horse remained popular until motorised machinery came in. Horses, of course, drew the ploughs – which were made locally by Harling of Sedgwick, Garnett of Endmoor, and Stainton of Milton (near Endmoor). This local interest produced a spate of ploughing matches. Agricultural shows, which included many different kinds of competition, became increasingly popular – the largest being the Westmorland County Show, originally held in Kendal, and today at Crooklands.

In the past farmers used any available type of dog to deal with sheep and cattle – lurchers, pointers, terriers and so on. All dogs had to be kept fastened up, as rabies was a danger, and dogs at large were destroyed. As with other domestic animals, dogs underwent special breeding for improvement. Dogs with special abilities – intelligence and expertise in shepherding – were bred. There were two main types, smooth-haired and rough-haired – the wonderful Border Collies so admired today.

The farmer's wife was often saddled with the care of poultry, and she might take surplus eggs to market for a bit of 'pin-money,' as is done today. Pig-rearing was never much of a feature of farming here, but usually a couple of pigs were kept, killed and cured for home consumption (I was brought up on a farm, and when we children got measles, the pigs were invariably also infected, with all the usual symptoms). At one time many non-farmers kept a few pigs and hens. They were fortunate if they had a garden in which to grow vegetables. Until the ravages of myxomatosis in the 1950s, rabbits were plentiful (as indeed they are once more). No doubt villagers' tables would occasionally be graced by more exotic dishes, pheasant or whatever, obtained by fair means or foul.

Farmers were ever plagued by the contagious diseases of farm animals – foot and mouth, pleuro-pneumonia, sheep scab, swine fever, anthrax and rabies. Thankfully these are rare now. Even as late as 1839, when foot and mouth broke out in South Westmorland, the 'need fire' was resorted to – to cure and prevent further trouble: this was doubtless a relic of fire-worship, handed down from aboriginal times. There was a local tradition that an angel was seen to descend and set fire to a tree. The strange sight attracted the curiosity of the cattle, and those affected were cured and remained immune ever after. Indeed – the angel left written instructions (!) – the fire was to be handed on from farm to farm and the cattle to be passed through the smoke. In the event of the need-fire going out, it was to be rekindled afresh by rubbing two pieces of wood together, wood that had never been in a house. All fires in houses had to be extinguished during the time of kindling. The last need-fire in this area was set alight in 1840 at Killington, not far from Natland. This was no doubt a talking point in Natland at that time: one by one, the old superstitions were being dispelled.

Numbers of Irishmen used to come over to work during hay-time and harvest, when extra help was needed. They were often happy to be accommodated in one of the farm buildings, and would be well fed. They would come year after year. Outlying farms, especially, were often visited by 'gentlemen of the road' – tramps. They were usually old, dirty and smelly. They knew where they would get food and a billy-can of hot tea. Often they wanted accommodation too, but there were strict rules about this: my father used to show them into a loft over the shippon, which was warm because the cows were underneath. They were asked for their box of matches (of course they always kept another box concealed), and told that they would be locked in so that they couldn't escape if they started a fire. Even so, at times we found that someone had slept on a 'hay-mow' (hay-stack), leaving behind an empty cigarette packet and other rubbish. This was often the cause of farm fires.

THE TURNPIKES

In the late eighteenth and early nineteenth centuries the roads were improved: not before time, one might add. An Act of Parliament of 1752 authorised the construction of turnpike roads in Westmorland. Before this the whole of trade was carried on by packhorses, travelling on mere tracks

The old Toll Bar

The Toll Bar in 1961

Courtesy late Mrs. Maples

only five or six feet wide, usually in bad repair and often under water. The first two turnpikes were soon constructed, Heron Syke to Eamont Bridge and Keighley to Kendal. Others followed, including Kendal to Milnthorpe in 1820. In 1757 the first carrier's stage wagon took hams, butter and fruit from Kendal to London – no doubt causing something of a sensation. As commons were enclosed and roads improved, single-horse carts were introduced in remoter districts: at first these were just a few boards on solid wheels, without sides, called 'clog-wheeled cars' or 'tumblers.' As late as 1843 dogs were sometimes attached helping to pull heavily laden carriages in Kendal, and letters of protest appeared in Kendal papers. An Act of Parliament made provision for the appointment of trustees for the turnpikes, with special property qualifications – a clear yearly value of rents and profits from land of £40. Money raised through tolls was to be used for repairing roads. Material for repairs could be taken, without payment, out of any brook, river, waste or common ground – or, if not sufficient, from any other land – but not a house or garden. The trustees could borrow money if necessary. There were exemptions from toll-paying. Individuals were still liable to 'statute' work on the roads, but were able to 'compound' (settle by a money payment). Milestones were to be erected by the trustees. The toll-bar on the way to Kendal was at the junction of what is now Natland Road and Burton Road, and the house still stands near the present-day roundabout.

Transport was reaching up to modernisation. The first stagecoach passed through Kendal in 1763, running twice a week – drawn by six horses at the rate of 6 mph. In 1786 the first mail-coach – on the important route from London to Edinburgh – passed through Kendal. I wonder how Natland folk viewed these wonderful things, and whether anyone from the village braved that journey. By 1825 there were eighteen to twenty coaches passing through Kendal daily (what a busy place!); but ten years later the numbers began gradually to decrease, until in 1849 there was only one, the old Leeds coach – and that ceased running soon afterwards. The railways were being built, and as a result journeys were greatly accelerated. In the meantime the Kendal to Lancaster Canal opened in 1819, carrying passengers, goods and produce, but its passenger packets ceased the day the railway opened – September 1st 1846. The canal continued to function for goods and, when it actually froze the following December, butter boxes were sent by rail; this traffic soon transferred to rail as it was cheaper than the canal.

In 1824 John McAdam was appointed Surveyor of Roads from Kendal to Penrith, and later Superintendent of Milnthorpe and Heron Syke turnpikes: 'macadamisation' was first carried on these roads in 1826. The farmers protested that their horses would be lamed. The cost of upkeep of turnpikes in 1834 was £17. 10s per mile – a great deal of money in those days. On

Natland Railway Bridge (Helm Lane)

Courtesy late Mrs. Maples

the formation of the County Council there were 247 miles 3 furlongs and 102 yards of main roads, and 195 bridges: these were handed over to the authority on March 25th 1889. Steamrollers were first used in Westmorland in 1886 – 10 tons on main roads and smaller ones for secondary roads. Natland's bridges are Hawes Bridge, Mill Beck High, Mill Beck Middle, and Mill Beck Low.

THE MARBLE QUARRY

There are still signs of an old marble quarry by the River Kent below Larkrigg Farm – a few huge blocks of limestone, abandoned many years ago. Similar limestone was extracted on Kendal Fell. Parson and White's Directory of 1829 notes that the marble works in Kendal and neighbourhood, 'belonging to George and Francis Webster, are very extensive, and were first brought into repute by the late Mr Webster, architect, who, about 30 years ago, constructed machinery on the River Kent, for sawing and polishing the marble' (pp. 638-39). I understand that the works were on the west side of the river, roughly opposite Watercrook Farm. No doubt some of the menfolk of Natland would be employed at the quarry by the river, and perhaps also at the processing works. Parson and White add that in Kendal 'Messrs. Webster have splendid show-rooms, for manufactured chimney-pieces, &c.;' the new canal, we are told, 'facilitates the importation of Italian marble, to be here manufactured and re-shipped to most of the principal towns in the kingdom;' the Kendal Fell limestone is 'very hard and beautiful, being variegated with petrified shells &c.' (p. 639). There must be many older residences in Kendal still containing handsome, locally made marble mantelpieces – unless they have been replaced by 'living flame' gas fires.

FIELD WALLS AND DRAINING

Natland's field walls, which are such a distinctive feature of the landscape, were mostly built of stones gathered from the fields; usually about 4 feet 6 inches high, they incorporate two sets of 'throughs,' and a 'cam' of flattish stones, sometimes of roughly dressed limestone, on top. They are, of course, dry-walled – that is, built without cement. If the farmer hired a waller, he would have to pay, in 1845, 8s per rod of 7 yards, including gathering and carting the stone. There was also draining to be done, and though local stone could be used if suitable, tiles were probably more effective. These were made like clay bricks, but in the form of short lengths of piping. Small local tile works developed, and Natland farmers would get theirs from the nearest works at Lupton. By the time Mr Garnett wrote his account there were no tile works left in Westmorland.

NATLAND'S OLD FARMHOUSES

With the exception of Natland Park, all the farms in Natland probably occupy sites that have been used since Norse times. Natland Hall and Cracalt may be the oldest houses. As we have seen, Natland Hall was granted a chapel in 1246, and there may well have been a house here since the earliest Norse settlement. The house has at some date been heightened: the RCHM survey (*An Inventory of the Historical Monuments in Westmorland*, p. 180) suggests that this took place in the eighteenth or nineteenth centuries, but I would guess earlier. The central chimney stack is of special interest, as it has two double canopy chimneys, unique in Westmorland. There are a panelled screen and panelled doors. The staircase is seventeenth-century, with turned balusters and square newels. The roof structure may be original. In the cellar there is some stonework which could be part of the very first building. Natland Hall formerly had a hatch through what had been an external wall of the kitchen, closed now by a building on the other side: the old beams can still be seen. It has been suggested that long ago beggars or the village poor might go to the hatch to be given food.

Cracalt Farmhouse must date back to a similar time as it is mentioned in early documents, with a variety of spellings: a deed of 1290, for example, mentions 'Nicholas de Crakehale,' bondman to Walter de Stirklaund, and a document of 1312 mentions the estate of 'Crakhal,' held by Robert de

Natland Hall.

Natland Hall from the bank.

Courtesy late Mrs. Maples

Wessington and his wife Joan (see above, 'Records of the Barony of Kendale'). The house doubtless developed on similar lines to Natland Hall, but as it stands today it seems to have lost all its ancient internal features.

Larkrigg, which was in Natland until about 1712, is mentioned in the deed of 1292 as 'Lowkerig.' High House has oval chimneys, some original window frames, and a cupboard with the date 1666 and initials 'TWE.' It has a late seventeenth-century staircase and some panelling. The west wing of Watercrook Farmhouse is possibly sixteenth-century; the house contains two seventeenth-century staircases, some panelling and a small cupboard with initials 'I.E.S.,' and the date 1631. The site of this farm may have been occupied continuously since Roman times, good sites being used and reused.

Natland Abbey has several interesting details. According to the RCHM survey (p.180), the present house was probably built in the mid-sixteenth century. It is of H-shaped plan, with cross-wings at the east and west ends. Inside the building are some seventeenth-century panelled doors, and a doorway with a flat four-centred head. The late seventeenth-century staircase has turned balusters and square newels with ball-terminals. The roofs of the main block and the east wing have curved principals and collars. (The Commission makes no mention of a hidey-hole, but there is one, a real one: I know, as I used to stay at the Abbey as a child, when my Uncle Aaron

Natland Abbey – East View.

Courtesy late Mrs. Maples

45

Ewan farmed there. There used to be William Morris wallpaper on the staircase.) Natland Abbey was never an abbey, but belonged to St. Mary's Abbey at York. It was common for abbeys, as great landlords in their own right, to maintain farms where lay brothers or agents administered the lands and collected tithes and rents. Some of these farms had important buildings, and where these have survived, are often dignified with the title 'abbey' or 'priory.'

Town End is another of Natland's old houses. In the spring of 1973 John Atkinson, the present owner, was having some alterations done, and kindly showed me round part of the house. An interior passage, paved with neat narrow cobbles, seemed to divide the building: the end nearest the road could possibly have been a barn, with the house at the other end – an example of what is referred to as a 'longhouse'farm. John told me about other features: there had, for instance, been a well on the south side. The 'outshot' at the back must itself be fairly old. There were pegged beams in the attic and the attic door had been 'adzed.' Some ARP helmets were found up there too, so perhaps Town End was the Wardens' centre during the Second World War.

Chapter 4

A CENTURY OF CHANGE

THE FIRST WORLD WAR AND AFTER

The twentieth century saw the most rapid changes in Natland's history. During the first two decades there were events of national importance. The death in 1901 of Queen Victoria, aged 81, the longest reigning monarch and longest lived of all British monarchs so far, was felt to mark the end of an era. Edward VII ascended the throne, to be succeeded by George V. The Boer War took place in South Africa, but I have found no evidence of its impact on Natland. The First World War (the 'Great War') certainly did touch the village. By 1919 the men who had defended our freedom were returning to their 'brave new world.' Of the 130 men from Natland parish, including the old boys of St. Mark's Home, six failed to return, and their names appear on the War Memorial in the churchyard: A. Cragghill, T. Elleray, J. Fallowfield, F. Inman, J. E. Inman and G. E. H. Keesey.

The *Westmorland Gazette* gives us a fascinating insight into life at this troubled time. The issue of January 11th 1919 contains a pathetic little notice:

> Wanted, information – Pte. J. Fallowfield, 24208. A.Company,
> 8th Border Regt., Reported missing March 23rd 1918.
> Will any returned prisoner-of-war knowing
> any information kindly communicate with his mother,
> Mrs Fallowfield, Church View, Natland.

The Westmorland War Agricultural Committee announced that, owing to the limited number of tractors available for the 1919 ploughing season, farmers requiring assistance were requested to send their applications for Tractor and Horse Ploughing teams immediately. There was to be a lecture in Kendal Town Hall on Potato Growing, and the importance of substituting them for corn, only certain varieties being allowed in scheduled areas. There was demobilisation of Army horses, on loan at £2 per year. Natland Abbey was to have a sale of Stock, Implements and Furniture. Bob Bindloss of Higher House Farm sold a calved cow at Kendal Auction for £55. Heavy horses were bringing anything from £86 to £170. Herdwick ewes were selling at 30s to 34s. At Kendal market oats were selling at 2s 2d, flour at 2s 8d a stone; ham was 2s 2d a pound, and salmon 4s. Crabs were 2s to 4s each, rabbits 2s 2d, chickens 8s to 10s, hens 6s to 8s. Eggs were 2½d each. Potatoes were 11d to 1s per stone. Many of the advertisements of that time were for firms remembered today, some continuing under different names: Crofts – Automobile Engineers; Webbs – Horticultural Stores; Musgroves

Mrs. Pooley Nelson

Mrs. Cook
Courtesy late Mrs. Maples

–Tailor-Made Costumes etc. (now Beales, though I doubt if they do any tailoring today). Alf Heap, Chemist and Optician, offered spectacles for 2s 6d, your sight tested free. The *Westmorland Gazette* itself cost only 2d. Always noted for its 'efforts,' Natland held a Whist Drive and Dance in aid of Soldiers' Comforts that spring – and raised £40, a considerable amount of money in those days.

In March of 1919 Bell's milk float plunged into the river in Kendal. Mr Bell was to farm Watercrook in later years. The little boy who had been thrown into the water was his son, Nat, known by many for his soulful rendering of songs from whichever musical was currently being rehearsed or performed by the Kendal Operatic Society: Nat was a member of the Chorus. When he was older he could also be heard singing these songs as he repaired the field walls. The *Westmorland Gazette* of May 3rd reported the wedding of Edith Ellen Conway of Helmside to James William Bryer of Spital View, a marriage which achieved over fifty golden years.

On May 10th a meeting took place in Natland School to consider the form of the Peace Celebrations. Medals or mugs for the children were considered unsuitable, as the children soon tired of them. Several suggestions were put forward, and the event that took place in August was conventional enough:

a short open-air service, sports for children and adults, tea all round, and a dance in the evening. During that summer four boys from St. Mark's swam across Windermere, from Fellborough to Storrs Hall Pier, making a total of twenty-two to have achieved this: this was apparently something which was 'done' at that time. In October life was temporarily disrupted by a railwaymen's strike, but this was called off the following week. At that time there were a surprising number of motor accidents considering the few vehicles on the roads, but, happily, none in Natland Parish.

In addition to whist drives, concerts and dances, one could cycle (or motor if one was lucky enough to have a car) to Kendal where one could see silent films. 'Adam Bede' and 'Within the Law' were on at St. George's Theatre, and the Kendal Kinema's programme included evocative titles such as 'Love's Miracle' (in five parts!), 'The Hooded Terror,' 'Stolen Honour' and 'The Bride of Fear.' These would hold no horrors for Natlanders, whose superstitious forefathers a century earlier had been haunted by a round dozen 'dobbies' (ghosts or spirits).

New Building

Few English villages, especially those situated close to a town, can have remained substantially unaltered through the twentieth century. Natland's proximity to Kendal, its excellent transport links – particularly after the construction of the M6 – and its pleasant situation on the gentle slopes between Helm and the River Kent, have all contributed to the village's modern residential development. Ask any old Natlander about the changes that have taken place here over the last forty years or so, and the answer is almost invariably 'all these new houses.' Less obvious has been the revolution in farming methods, and, of no less importance, the loss of several farms as viable units (I think this is very sad).

Just off the village Green there had been the old 'Horse and Farrier' Inn, now the village shop and Post Office. In 1921 the property was bought by Jim Douthwaite, an odd-job man, who converted the adjoining stables into a house. One of Natland's old ladies lived there in the 60s, Mrs Pooley Nelson – who had a wonderful store of local lore. About the same time Jim Douthwaite built two houses, semi-detached, on what had been the drying ground for the laundry across the way. The laundry itself, now Compton House, had been a joiner's shop at one time, and there was a tradition that religious meetings had taken place there. This was almost certainly the site of the early chapel granted to Natland Hall in 1292. The laundry itself was eventually converted into a pair of dwellings, in one of which lived an old lady, Mrs Cook, who was said to be a descendant of the gypsy families who had made their headquarters in Natland many years ago. Since then the

Early 1930-40s outside the PO, with old van (possibly laundry) parked outside Compton House.
Courtesy John Marsh Collection

Park Close at the time of road widening in 1968.
New houses, Charnley Close, have now been built opposite.   Courtesy Bill Moffat

house has been converted back to a single dwelling. In 1922 a gardener's lodge was built at Windy Brow, now Grassgarth, and two years later Mr Atkinson Moorhouse converted some of the Lower House barns into a pair of semis, now known as Crosby Lodge and Bield.

Oxenholme, close to the main road and the railway, saw a good deal of new building in the years after the First World War. Building of the Rural District Council's Bolefoot estate was begun in 1921 and completed two years later. The first bungalow in Natland, Hillclose, was built by Mr and Mrs Hodgson near the railway bridge on Helm Lane. Just before the Second World War one of their family, Mrs George, and her family built another bungalow, Lea Green, on the south side of the village Green. About the same time a terrace of private houses was erected at Oxenholme. Between the two Wars several new houses appeared in the lanes leading off from the Green. In 1947 the Council built eight houses called Park Close, just round the corner, by the side of the Kendal road, with four more, alongside, three years later. For many years these were referred to as 'the new houses.' But the greatest burst of activity came in the early 60s after the long-awaited sewerage system was installed: Natland was up-to-date at last!

REFUSE COLLECTION AND SEWERAGE

At the beginning of the twentieth century drainage in Natland had been primitive, to put it mildly, and the powers-that-be very tardy in making improvements. A limited service of refuse collection, including the emptying of privies and privy ashpits, began in the village late in 1915: up to that time, apparently, the Council had regarded it as the duty of each householder to dispose of the family refuse. In Westmorland as elsewhere the military call-up during the First World War no doubt brought with it increased anxieties about the state of public health. For some time the service was carried out by contractors. It is difficult to say when a refuse collection was started in Oxenholme, as the old records usually do not distinguish between the two parts of the civil parish; but it seems likely that a limited service was begun about the same time. Only in 1923, when the Bolefoot Council houses were built, was a service on any scale provided for Oxenholme. I came across the following minute passed by the Public Health Committee of the Rural District Council on 4th February, 1933:

> Oxenholme Refuse
> On a recommendation of the Natland Parochial Committee,
> it was resolved – that the contents of the ashbins in Oxenholme
> area be removed by direct labour, the refuse to be disposed of at
> the Kendal Corporation's tip at a cost of 2/- per load.

The first sewerage and sewage disposal scheme provided in Oxenholme was

Family photograph of Sam, John, Robert and Whin in front of School House in 1949.

Telephone: KENDAL 1408

J. W. MOFFAT

Agricultural Contractor

★ PICK-UP BALING

★ THRESHING

★ PLOUGHING

★ LIME SPREADING

NATLAND   KENDAL

Advertisement in the 1959 NFU Telephone Directory.   Courtesy Bill Moffat.

a septic tank disposal system for the drainage of the Bolefoot Council houses. This system became the subject of complaints (presumably about overflowing contents), and some improvements were carried out in 1926-27. Whilst the system was constructed at the expense of the housing scheme, it was subsequently maintained as a public sewerage system. It became the responsibility of Kendal Borough Council from 1st April 1935. In the mid-1950s the village had been told that the long-promised sewerage scheme had 'slipped down the list of priorities.' In 1969 I was informed in a letter from the Rural District Council that:

> What is known as the design stage of the proposed sewerage and sewage disposal scheme for Natland is well advanced, and a provisional agreement has been reached for the purchase of the land required for the disposal works. I am hoping that before the end of this year the Council will be able to make application to the Minister of Housing and Local Government for approval to invite tenders, and for consent to borrow the sum of money required for the construction of the works. The only outstanding matter before that action can be taken is the negotiations which are about to be commenced with Westmorland County Council for a grant-in-aid. But these could take anything up to three months, as the County authority does not meet very often. When the Council eventually are able to go to the Ministry, they then face the task of establishing to their (the Ministry's) satisfaction that the need for, and the urgency of, the scheme are such that it could not be postponed to meet the call of the Government for restriction of public expenditure in the interests of the national economy.

Despite all the complications this letter seemed moderately reassuring: shortly afterwards work on the sewerage scheme began.

When my husband became Headmaster of Natland School in 1945, the School House was occupied; but by spring 1948 we were able to move in, with some trepidation. The toilet was in a small building abutting what is now the village hall. It had a bucket, with a wooden seat over. The bucket was emptied weekly, and if memory serves me right, this was along with the ashbin, all in one refuse cart. This arrangement was especially unsatisfactory during the frequent invasions of relatives and friends, when the bucket would often overflow. (What a disgusting mess we had to clean up!) Our visitors said they came to enjoy the lovely countryside, but we had a feeling that our primitive privies were an added interest and talking point on their return to more civilised parts. Those buckets were actually supposed to be an advance on the older earth closets, which required daily applications of ashes from the grate. At least they didn't overflow at crucial moments.

Old Smithy, Church View.

Courtesy late Mrs. Maples

Shanny Hutchinson and prize winning cow in Jockey Field.

Courtesy late Mrs. Maples

The drainage for newer properties was by septic tank: there was generally one to each house, but the Park Close houses had communal tanks. There may still have been one or two cesspools – I don't know. Due to the peculiar lie of the land at Park Close, the Council had to come to their aid frequently, and Mr Moffat of Hawes Lane had a fair sideline in the pumping trade: the spreading of 'tank' on the fields always seemed to take place upwind. But in spite of seeping septic tanks and the occasional none-too-fresh air in those days, we had an undeniable tradition of longevity in Natland. The 1961 census assured us that the age distribution of Westmorland was older than that of the country as a whole. Today, in 2006, Natlanders regularly reach their nineties. This may, of course, be the survival of the fittest. But I'm sure that the wholesome combination of modern sewerage and the regular weekly collection of refuse, by specially designed vehicles collecting mechanically from vermin-proof 'wheelie bins,' has had a beneficial effect on our health.

THE 1960S AND AFTER: NEW HOUSING ESTATES

The large-scale expansion of Natland began in the mid-1960s. Natland Abbey farm buildings were demolished, and the adjoining land built up as Abbey Drive with thirteen dwellings, followed by Robbie Lea Drive, on the other side of the lane, with eleven, all of these being bungalows or semi-bungalows. When the old village School on the Green was demolished in 1967, it was replaced by a new building just round the corner on Oxenholme Lane, the old site being filled in by three houses, one single dwelling and a pair of semis. By 1974 the development of further bungalows and semi-bungalows on Shanny Lane, Long Meadow Lane, and Wandales Lane had been completed. In the 80s there was more development, Abbey Gardens on the east side of Holmes' Nursery Gardens, and the flats and cottages of Town End Court which filled in the space between Holmes' and the old property of Town End (the barn that stood there had at one time housed the village smithy). A group of small cottages on the west side of the Green were converted into two dwellings, keeping their cottagey appearance. (I wonder whether these cottages, when built, were encroachments on the Green?) More houses at St Mark's Fold completed Natland's twentieth-century development. The twenty-first century brought yet further village expansion with a new estate, Charnley Fold, opposite Park Close, on Natland Hall land. There have also been several housing developments up at Oxenholme.

How were the new streets named? Abbey Drive was close to Natland Abbey, and Long Meadow Lane was partly built on a field called Long Meadow. Wandales Lane headed for what had been the open fields. The field name Robbie Lea, preserved in the street name Robbie Lea Drive, got its name from a previous owner. Shanny Lane was suggested as a memorial to Nathaniel Hutchinson, known to all as Shanny. He lived from 1857 to 1932, the son of Thomas Hutchinson of Higher House Farm. On his marriage he farmed the land next to the school, living at the house now called Greenside. The farm buildings have been converted into housing. For over fifty years he was Parish Clerk. He supplied the villagers with milk, brought their coal from Oxenholme, killed their pigs, – and, better still, arranged their weddings and burials. At one time Oxenholme Lane was known as Shanny Lane, and the corner near Greenside as Shanny's Corner.

I have been unable to find any housing prices for the early developments, but by the late 30s a new terraced house at Oxenholme was costing £320. This same house would change hands for many times that figure today. Natland house prices are very high today, often reaching or exceeding the dizzying figure of a quarter of a million – pounds, not shillings or pence. Some of the larger houses, such as Helme Lodge, where the Crewdson family used to live, have been converted into stylish flats. Older houses have been modernised to rival their newer neighbours. Most property is purchased on a mortgage, usually a financial burden for the young. People have moved to Natland from far and wide, some to work locally, some for retirement. Before the great development of the village took place, everybody knew everybody else, but this is certainly no longer the case. On the other hand, the newcomers frequently bring new interests and ideas, enriching the life of the community. I think we have mostly escaped the weekend cottage trend that has spoiled so many villages near the Lake District: but who can blame city dwellers for staking their small claim in such delightful surroundings?

POPULATION STATISTICS

Thomas Machell recorded that when he visited Natland in the early 1690s there were about thirty families living here: this figure may include some of the gypsy families, as it was in April when he visited, and the gypsies might still have been in residence.

The sources for the following population figures are the Cumbria County Record Office in Kendal, and the Office for National Statistics, Information and Intelligence. In 1841 there were 225 persons living in 39 houses, being 123 males and 102 females; and in 1851 there were 226 persons living in 39 houses, being 103 males and 123 females. Seventy years later, in 1921, there were 572 persons living in an area of 1,156 acres, including 20 acres of water. There was an almost equal ratio of males and females, living in 119 separate dwellings, and occupying 631 rooms. The average age over the whole of the Rural District was 32.0 for males and 33.3 for females. The National Census of 1921 reports the general superiority of accommodation in rural parts compared with urban areas. In 1956 there were 623 parishioners, including 168 children; 168 women were working outside the home, and there were 42 agricultural workers, 39 railway workers, and 114 people, male and female, working in Kendal. In 1961 there were 351 persons living on 892 acres, in 107 separate dwellings, occupying 529 rooms. There was little difference of ratio between males and females. In 1969 there was an estimated population, including Oxenholme, of about 1,000, taking into account recent building, and in spite of smaller families. In 1991, in Natland alone, there were 677 persons, and four years later, again in Natland alone, there were 716 persons. The age structure in 1995 was as follows:

aged	0-14	132
aged	15-29	118
aged	30-44	164
aged	45-59	141
aged	60-74	104
aged	75-84	48
aged	85 +	10

WATER SUPPLY

Many years ago all the Natland farms would have their own water supply: a water supply would indeed be one of the reasons for occupation. At one time there was a pump on the edge of the village green just opposite Mrs George's bungalow, Lea Green. Sometime in the 60s the Council needed to open up the well, and according to Mrs George it was still in good order. Other old wells, of course, may still be lying undiscovered. Years ago when Mr and Mrs Johnson were building their garage at Lower House, a well was uncovered at the foot of the wall behind the garage site. As late as the 1940s, when Edward Kendal and family lived there, there was still a pump in working order at Natland Park Farm. The village pumps were superseded by piped water from springs on Helm, but after many years this was found to be unsatisfactory and at some date unknown, Natland was connected to the Lupton Reservoir supply, and also linked to the Thirlmere-Manchester pipeline for times of drought: in 1924 the Parish Council noted that Thirlmere water was being increasingly resorted to at 1s per 1,000 gallons. There were the odd occasions, years ago, usually coinciding with a big sheet-wash, when something akin to weak tomato soup gushed from the cold tap, while at other times we had something resembling aerated water, in appearance if not in taste. We now take all our water from the Thirlmere supply, and very good water it is. Oxenholme's water comes from Fisher Tarn, belonging to Kendal Borough. Compared with other parts of the country, where shortages are increasingly frequent, restrictions on the use of water are rare.

Helmeside Road with the new railway houses – note scaffolding across the road at the Mission Hall. Left: Mr. and Mrs. Thompson, Mrs. Thornborrow, Mrs. Speed, Mrs. Schofield, Mrs. Machell. Right: Mrs. Elizabeth Robinson with Lilian, Alf and Ethel. Mrs. Dunlop's mother Mrs. Nelson in doorway with dog. Mrs. Pinch and Phyllis and Vincent. Mrs. ? and Queenie (went to USA).

J. Anderson, Kendal.

HEALTH

There has always been a good choice of doctors, though before the National Health Scheme was brought in (1948), a doctor would only be summoned in real need. At Helmside in days gone by, in case of illness a board was placed at the end of the road, so that Dr Brumwell would stop in his horse and trap, on his way from Kendal to Endmoor. In urgent cases he would call immediately; otherwise he would bring along the appropriate medicine. Until, and indeed after, the formation of the local Nursing Association in 1921, the normal ministrations were performed by women 'who did these things.' There was a Mrs Townley, a widow with quite a large family to keep, who could turn her hand to anything – helping at births, deaths and so on.

Formed in 1921, the Old and New Hutton and Natland Nursing Association appointed their first 'District Nurse' in February 1922: this was Nurse Heap, who lived in New Hutton. She made her rounds on a push-bike at first: in 1924 a motor-bike was purchased for her, which must have made it much easier to get about. She could use a taxi for very urgent cases in bad weather. Two years later the Association bought a second-hand Trojan car for Nurse Heap. Her salary was £150 per annum. Fêtes were held in each of the parishes in turn, to raise funds: the first, held in Natland, raised £31. 16s. 7d. Preliminary grants were given to get the Association on its feet – the County Council giving £10, the Red Cross £100, and the Education and Health Department £60. There was a constant worry that fêtes and subscriptions might fail to meet costs.

Nurse Heap left in 1928, and was followed by Nurse Thornborrow, who lived at 9 Bolefoot, Oxenholme. During her long service here, which continued till 1959, Nurse Thornborrow must have assisted at many births and attended many deaths, as well as carrying out other duties. She was to see many changes. In 1930 our local Association became affiliated to the newly formed Westmorland County Nursing Association, and by 1933 the County Council was taking on much of the financial burden. The local Committee gratefully accepted a new car. Meetings of the Committee were held at the Station Inn: prominent Natland members were Mrs Crewdson of Helme Lodge, Mrs Page of Brough Fold, Mrs Somerville, and later Mrs Keesey. The Secretary was Mrs Anson of Windy Brow (now Grassgarth). The Committee met four times a year. The annual subscription was 5s for cottages and 10s for bigger houses; the charge for midwifery was 10s if the doctor was present, and £1 if the nurse had to manage on her own. Non-members paid 2s for a first visit, 1s for a second visit, but no more than two visits were allowed unless they joined as members. The County Council took over completely on July 5th 1948. This must have been a relief to those who had the responsibility of raising funds. And a doctor was then available without regard to cost!

Nurse Thornborrow retired to keep house for her brother at Bowston, near Burneside. I must mention that as District Nurse she performed various duties for the gypsies who still regularly visited the area, camping on Little Helm: she was indeed a good friend to them. When necessary she assisted at a birth, and she used to remark that their bed linen was absolutely snow-white. And whenever they came this way they looked her up and gave her a supply of their special clothes pegs.

During the Second World War special provision was made to safeguard children's health. For expectant mothers cod liver oil, later in tablet form, was available free of charge; for babies there were cod liver oil and orange juice, the latter at 5d per bottle. At first these were collected from Kendal Town Hall – where ration books also had to be collected – and later from the Kendal Parish Hall. Without a car this meant a pram-pushing expedition – not easy. After the War supplies for babies were obtainable at the Clinic in Stramongate, where we could also have our babies weighed. More pram-pushing, especially difficult if there was a toddler to look after in addition to the baby in the pram. Usually two or three mums, each pushing her pram, would undertake the expedition together.

For serious cases there is the Westmorland General Hospital on Burton Road, and a few cases are taken to Lancaster. The Helme Chase maternity wing, where most local babies are born, replaced the old Helme Chase Maternity Hospital. The National Health Service, started so enthusiastically and hopefully in 1948, has gradually been debased by recourse to privatisation. Investors have to be paid their interest, and this inevitably means loss of funding to the country's hospitals and services. Not only that, but, at the time of writing, vast sums are being taken to keep an illegal war going. As in other parts of the country, our own local hospital is currently threatened with ward closures – wards we cannot let go. It is sad that we have lost sight of the promise of care 'from the cradle to the grave!'

PARISH COUNCIL

For several centuries the responsibility of keeping law and order, and the maintenance of the poor, had rested with the village Constables, Guardians and Overseers, people usually of some standing; in some cases offices were held by rota, and sometimes they were combined. In 1834 parishes had been compulsorily amalgamated into 'unions for administration of affairs of the poor and the vagrant.' Parish Councils had been established by the Local Government Act of 1894. Only the Overseers are mentioned in the minutes of our Natland Parish Council: this officer was elected annually, and in 1920 he was paid £20 a year, plus expenses. The duties of an Overseer were many – the preparation of valuation lists, jury lists, obligations concerned with censuses, the provision of work for those unable to find it themselves, the giving of poor relief in emergencies, and so on. With the national reorganisation of local government in the mid-20s, many of the responsibilities of the Parish Councils were taken over by the Counties, and the Overseers were no longer needed. In Natland the Overseer was no longer mentioned after 1928.

Colonel Crewdson, of Helme Lodge, was Chairman of the Parish Council and Parochial Church Council for fifty years! Mr William Cartmell served a similarly long period as Parish Clerk up till 1958. He and his wife lived in the cottage up Helm Lane where Mrs Cartmell had lived all her life. For many of those years he held a variety of other offices such as Rate Collector, Rent Collector, local reporter for the *Westmorland Gazette*, etc. Whatever went on in Natland, Mr Cartmell was sure to be involved in some capacity. Our Parish Council does not seem to have met with any regularity, but it apparently functioned well. Some of their dealings were quite amusing – or were they? In May of 1919 a letter had been received from the offices of the Clerk of the Peace and County Council headed 'Rats Order 1918.' The County Council scheme for the wholesale destruction of rats throughout the county was in full working order in most parishes except Natland: this was due to the fact that Natland had not appointed any person to receive rats' tails and issue certificates for payment. They were to take immediate action. We are not told who was appointed, but they likely did take action, as nothing more was heard on the subject. As early as 1923 there were complaints about the mess that the gypsies made on Little Helm, or Sinkfalls as it is sometimes known.

In 1935 there was a review of our parish footpaths, and they were listed as follows:

1. From Helm Lane over 2 stiles to Sedgwick Road.
2. From Helm Lane across the railway, over 1 stile and by 1 lane to the Kirkby Lonsdale Road.
3. From the canal bridge in Hawes Lane, by 1 stile and 1 gate to Cracalt Farm.
4. From the Natland to Kendal road at Haggdale Field, through the gardens ['Rigg's Garden'] to this side of the canal bridge.
5. From Higher House to the railway and out at the main road at Helmside. [This was later diverted at the lower end when Shanny Lane was built].
6. From this side of Hawes tip [a few yards up-river from Hawes Bridge, where rubbish used to be dumped] along the River Kent to Watercrook and out at Kendal Grammar School.
7. From Burton Road at Windy Brow [later Grassgarth] down lane on opposite side, through field to Mill Cottage, Oxenholme Farm.

Coronation Bonfire Organisers. Left to right: Jim Frearson, Jimmy Edmondson, Edwin Howson, Libby Moffat, Billy Brown, Mrs. Keesey, Alan and Arthur Brown.
Back row: Peter Bowden, Johnny Walker, Keith Hine, Audrey Moffat, Jack Howson and Jack Moffat.
Courtesy Bill Moffat

Early picture of Helm.
Courtesy Margaret Duff Collection

8. From St. Mark's Home [now Appletree School] past Cracalt Farm to High Cockrow Wood.
9. From the School House along fields to Natland Park Farm.
10. From Hawes Bridge through fields to Robin Hood's Wood and the Old Weir.

In 1965, when these footpaths were being checked, it was decided that No. 3 should not be reopened, as it had fallen into disuse. At that time also, footpaths 1 and 5 had to be cleared somewhat.

The Parish Council has been instrumental in organising the village's activities on all great occasions. For the Silver Jubilee of King George V and Queen Mary in 1935 there were sports, tea, a whist drive, and a bonfire on Helm. Two years later, at the Coronation of King George VI and Queen Elizabeth, a similar programme was organised, though with no bonfire, and the whist drive was followed by a dance. All the children under five were given a beaker, and everyone over sixty had a free tea. A red hawthorn tree was planted on the Green, on the site of the old Natland Thorn, round which the gypsies had danced at the fairs so long ago. Miss Miller, daughter of Canon Miller, could remember the earlier tree as being very decrepit, and thought it had stood there till only a short time before the new one was planted.

During the War years the Parish Council formed a Fire Squad, and appointed a local Salvage Officer to collect waste paper etc. Another important celebration followed – the end of the War: there were sports, a tea party, and a whist drive and dance. Then, in June 1953, came the Coronation of Queen Elizabeth II. The ceremony itself was watched by villagers on a rented large-screen set in the school; there was a service in the Church, the planting of an oak tree from Windsor Great Park, and a bonfire on Helm with fireworks, not forgetting a meat tea for 300 adults and children. Inscribed prayer books were presented to all the village children. There was a surplus from the large amount of money collected house-to-house and raised through whist drives, and with this two seats were placed, one on Helm, the other on the Green. A donation was also given to the King George Memorial Fund, a tea urn was purchased for public use, the oak tree was fenced, and there was still some money left to buy some folding chairs for public use.

There was discussion over the years about possible measures for the safety of pedestrians, particularly Oxenholme school children, on the stretch of main road from Helmside to the top of Oxenholme Lane. This was resolved when the major improvements were completed up there, with provision of a good footpath. For many years, as we have already seen, the Parish Council had only disappointing replies to their enquiries about a sewerage scheme.

Enough said about that. In the later 1960s there was talk of Natland being no longer coupled with Underbarrow as a County Council unit, but being joined with Old Hutton, New Hutton, Stainton and Sedgwick, as the 'Helm Division.'

In March 2004 the booklet 'Natland Parish Plan' was produced in response to the Countryside Agency's 'Vital Villages' initiative, of which parish plans were a major element. A distinguishing feature of this plan is the effort that has gone into finding out what most people really want for their parish. Mr David Peters is the current Chairman of the Parish Council, and Mrs Audrey Ireland, Secretary: living right beside the village Green she can keep an eye on all that goes on. At the next level of local government, the South Lakeland District Council, Brenda Gray (Liberal Democrat) is Councillor for Natland Ward, which includes Helsington, Sedgwick, Hincaster and Stainton. Our representative on the Cumbria County Council is Alan Bobbett (Conservative). Natland is, of course, part of the Westmorland and Lonsdale Parliamentary Constituency. Kendal was traditionally a Liberal stronghold, and in the General Election of 2005 Westmorland and Lonsdale went Liberal Democrat again, electing Tim Farron as our new parliamentary representative.

POLICE

Within the memory of Natlanders, the village was policed from Endmoor, with help from the Kendal Force when needed, which was seldom, as Natland was always law-abiding. There has been the odd incident, invariably trouble brought in from elsewhere. For a number of years, from 1951 to 1965, PC Crewdson, 'Crewdy' as he was nicknamed, served our area – Endmoor, Old Hutton and Natland. He made his way round on a bicycle for years, but latterly rode a motorbike. One of his jobs was checking on sheep dipping. He was succeeded by various PCs, including PC Blackett and PC Fishwick. The local Force was for many years the Cumberland and Westmorland Constabulary. Carlisle was incorporated about 1964, and about 1968 there was another change of name to the Cumbria Constabulary. We now have Kendal Rural Policing, based at Milnthorpe Police Station: the team consists of sixteen Constables, three Sergeants and an Inspector, covering the area from Kendal east to the Yorkshire and Lancashire borders, including the Grange area. Natland has its voluntary Neighbourhood Watch Scheme, which seems to be effective in helping to deter crime.

Chapter 5

COMMUNICATIONS

ROADS

Today Natland can boast excellent communications. The parish lies athwart a main road, the A65, and a main railway line (not quite as reliable since privatisation). The village is close to a second main road, the A6. We are lucky to have the M6 motorway easily accessible at junctions 36 on the A65 at Farleton, and 37 on the A684 north of Killington. To cope with the increasing volume of traffic our local roads have been improved, with awkward corners straightened and footpaths constructed where necessary. Years ago there were notices on Oxenholme Lane and Helm Lane indicating that they were to become 'streets.' Now how does a country lane become a street? With houses in close proximity there wasn't room to widen, so we waited, but nothing happened. When the road from Helmside to Oxenholme Station was being improved, Mr and Mrs Balmer and their daughter Wendy were transferred to a house on Bolefoot, as their house at the end of the terrace at Helmside was demolished to improve visibility at the road junction.

In 1962, due mainly to the efforts of Pearson Charnley, the crossroads on the Green were broken up and grassed over, and whitewashed stones, now replaced by kerbs, were placed round the edges to prevent cars parking on the grass. The Green is a lovely place for the children to play. Before 1920 the Green was used as the School playground, but that year it was decided

The Green before it was altered.

Courtesy late Mrs. Maples

to confine the scholars to the School yard because of traffic dangers! Eventually land behind the School was purchased to provide a playground. In 1900 some of the scholars had been taken by the Headmaster 'up to the high road to see the cars pass:' they would have been surprised to see the endless streams of traffic using the road a hundred years later.

When the Natland to Kendal road was improved and widened about 1968, the Council mercifully preserved the two old oak trees just north of the village. Young native trees – oak, ash, hawthorn, bird cherry, mountain ash, hazel, holly, field maple, wild cherry and blackthorn – were given by Mr Wilson of Larkrigg (they were saplings from the Larkrigg woods), and planted by Mr James, the Roads and Bridges Forester at that time, on the newly widened grass verges. Most of them grew happily, but a few were apparently deliberately destroyed. Along the road to Kendal, just past the oak trees but on the right hand side, is the field called Haggdale. At one time it was known to all as Rigg's Garden. This was something of a landmark: if one was walking into town, one could usually expect to be offered a lift before one reached Rigg's Garden, and if one was walking back, one felt at that point that one was nearing home. Lilian Wilkinson, who lived at Lowfield, told me that her grandfather, Thomas John Medcalfe, had been brought up by a stepfather by the name of Rigg, and the family used that name throughout life except for documents of birth, marriage and death. He had bought Haggdale many years before to work as a market garden, and his son Fred followed in his footsteps. In Kendal this Medcalfe family were known as Rigg, and in Natland by their rightful name, but the garden was always known as Rigg's. After Mr Medcalfe's death the field lay unused for a while until bought by Mr Wilson of Natland Park in 1968. It was cleared of garden and glasshouse remains and ploughed. Further along the road to Kendal, there used to be a bridge over the canal known locally as Dilly Bridge, supposedly after a little girl called Dilly, perhaps a member of the Crewdson family, who had drowned there. Hawes Lane, running down over the old canal bridge to Hawes Bridge, used to be a pleasant walk in days gone by, its hedgerows providing shelter for the first dog's mercury and celandines. Today it carries considerable traffic, and walking there is less of a pleasure.

I haven't been able to discover when Natland's roads were first tarred. Tarmacadam was being used earlier on main roads, but lesser roads consisted of little more than broken stones compacted by steamroller. Stones picked up from the surrounding fields during cultivation were piled up on roadsides, and these were broken up by the stone-breaker, usually an elderly man unable to do other work.

Bus Services

Oxenholme has always had a good bus service, but Natland hasn't fared as well. In the early years there was competition between local operators, some of which amalgamated and were acquired by the Ribble Company in 1927. Ribble expanded further with the takeover of the Kendal Motor Company in 1930. In December 1950 Dallam Motors of Milnthorpe, which had provided a bus service for Natland, was also taken over. Many years ago I went to see Mr Fawcett, who had founded the Dallam Motors in 1924, and was able to supply some information. Dallam ran a fleet of ten buses, operating a service between Kendal and Milnthorpe via Natland and Sedgwick: this originally ran on Mondays and Saturdays, then for many years on Saturdays only. Mr Glenden, a Ribble Company inspector, gave me a few details of bus fares and timetables. In 1949 the fare from Natland to Kendal was 4d single and 7d return, with half fare for children of 3 to 14 years. For a short time during the 1950s Natland had Wednesday buses also, but these were withdrawn because of lack of support. The Women's Institute made further representations to Ribble, and about 1967 we were again given a Wednesday service, though at the same time the Saturday service was cut back. Today the regular service to Helmside and Oxenholme has two alternating routes, 41 and 41A, one returning by the top road, so that agile folk can catch a bus at the top of Oxenholme Lane. Oxenholme people rarely travel to Kendal by rail these days, but in past times there was a general exodus on Saturday mornings by the 8.30 train.

The Railway: Oxenholme Station

The Lancaster to Carlisle railway was opened in December 1846. From 1859 to 1923 the main line to Scotland was known as the London and North Western Railway, then as the London, Midland and Scottish Railway till 1947, when it became part of the nationalised, prosaically titled British Railways (London Midland Region). At present services are run by Virgin Trains. Till 1872 the road from Kendal to Kirkby Lonsdale crossed the railway by a level crossing, but in that year an Act of Parliament permitted the London and North-Western Railway Company to divert it. To house the railway workers Oxenholme and Helmside were built, Helmside being completed in 1885, Natland Terrace and Hill Place in 1895 – with greater regard for landmark than landscape with their red brick construction so foreign to this area. Along the road to the station there used to be allotments, carefully cultivated by the railway workers, but these disappeared under later housing development. At the outbreak of the Second World War the glass was removed from the platform canopies at Oxenholme Station, for reasons of safety. Women took on jobs as clerks and

L & NWR (changed to LMS) 4.4.2.T. No. 6794 at Oxenholme on Windermere line ('local')
R.V. 152 Class 'Precurser 3P'. Note 16th February 1938 running bunker first.
Courtesy Margaret Duff Collection

Oxenholme Junction in 1914.

J. Simcoe   *Courtesy Margaret Duff Collection*

porters, and through the station flowed a constant stream of war traffic, men and materials. Oxenholme has always been a busy main-line junction, with the familiar announcement 'Change here for Kendal and Windermere.' The 50s and 60s brought many changes. The first diesel train ran on trial in February 1951, foreshadowing a new era in the life of the railway, and the diesels gradually superseded the old steam engines so beloved by generations of train spotters. The last steam-powered train ran in August 1968: gone was the thrill of watching for the steam expresses such as the 'Royal Scot' and the 'Caledonian.'

About 1919 or soon afterwards, as the men returned from the First World War, sixty-two men worked in the Oxenholme engine shed, which housed twenty-three locomotives in summer and fifteen in winter. In 1962 the sheds were closed down, and the station staff was reduced. After 1962 the Victorian refreshment room was closed and demolished, but some years later a new, much smaller waiting-refreshment room was built, which continues to function today. In 1966 the station even lost its Station Master – and what is a Railway Station without a Master? Control was taken over by an area manager at Penrith, and more recently by Carlisle. The railway houses were sold off. Way back in the late 60s, I can remember Mr Billy Kitchin telling me that he'd been a linesman for twenty-three years, and was

Oxenholme Staff 1956. T. Cornthwaite (Ticket Collector), James Tallon (Porter),
W. Rigby (Station Foreman), Mr. Archer (Station Master), and William Slater (Shunter).
Courtesy late Mrs. Maples

Trainspotters at Oxenholme Station.

Courtesy late Mrs. Maples

going to be made redundant shortly, along with about ten of his mates. In 1965 there was even a change of staff uniform, with the introduction of a 'continental' look. There were also changes in the colour of train coaches. I'm sure those staunch members of staff, Mr Bateson and Mr Balmer, must have been horrified as their beloved railway station changed so dramatically.

A lesser-known service provided by the railway had always been the telegraph, but about the same time this ceased to be a public service, and was only used for wiring railway information. Taking modernisation still further, the old wooden sleepers were replaced by concrete, with long-welded rails to cater for high-speed trains. The line underwent another drastic overhaul when it was electrified in 1974. The Oxenholme to Windermere route was reduced to a single line, which was a short-sighted move, adding to pressure on the roads into the Lake District.

There have been exciting times at Oxenholme Station when famous expresses have raced through – and times of horror too. Early one morning in February 1965, three policemen were searching for a gunman after an incident in Kendal during the night. The station must have felt eerie when they found their man in the waiting room at 3.15 am. He shot his way past them, killing one and wounding the other two. Reinforcements of police sealed off the roads and a desperate chase followed: eventually, at noon, the gunman was cornered on the far side of Helm. Even though we knew we were in no danger down in the village, we housewives locked our doors. We could see the figures of the police with their dogs moving over the hill, with the helicopter flying above them. In a horrible echo of this incident, a fatal stabbing occurred on May 27th 2006 in a southbound express near Oxenholme. A young man was arrested close to the station and later charged with murder.

THE CANAL

The canal predated the building of the railway, but its impact on local life was less important; it was, of course, the arrival of the railway that eventually made the canal redundant. The canal was the only navigable waterway in the area (though today the Kent bears the occasional brood of young canoeists). During the latter half of the eighteenth century the discovery of rich coalfields round Wigan coincided with the beginnings of industrialisation. The expansion of the industrial towns of South Lancashire created a demand for building stone, and land improvements in the Fylde area required large quantities of lime. The Kendal area could supply both, and also needed coal. A canal, offering cheap transport, would make possible a profitable two-way traffic. In 1771 traders and merchants of Lancaster had made preliminary attempts to build a canal, but it was not until 1792, when John Rennie was appointed Engineer to the newly formed Lancaster Canal Corporation, that an Act of Parliament was passed, and construction commenced. The canal took thirty years to complete. Water was brought from Killington Reservoir, which when completed in 1819 was the largest canal reservoir in the country, holding 761 million gallons of water. The line of the canal was originally planned to run from Wigan to Kendal, crossing the River Ribble at Preston, and the Lune at Lancaster, by aqueducts. The Lune aqueduct, for which Rennie was engineer, was completed in 1797, and remains sound to this day, but the Ribble aqueduct, which would have required numerous locks, proved too costly and was never built. The link was completed by the construction of a tramway from Preston, crossing the Ribble by bridge; but this proved too great an obstacle, and it was closed in 1851, severing the connection between the Wigan coalfields and the northern lime quarries.

One of the most impressive works was Rennie's Hincaster tunnel, 358 yards long, passing under one of the rounded glacial hills between Natland and Stainton. It was well engineered, and is still in wonderful condition. The tunnel was lined with about four million bricks, which were made locally from clay dug at Mosside farm, close to the canal itself. The barges were sometimes hauled through by a chain, and sometimes 'walked' through by the feet of the bargemen, paddling their feet against the roof of the tunnel

LANCASTER CANAL.

NOTICE IS HEREBY GIVEN, that the Canal from Lancaster to Kendal is intended to be opened for general Trade, on FRIDAY, the 18th day of June, 1819 *(not on Thursday, the 17th, as was previously advertized)*; and that PACKET BOATS will be established, for the conveyance of Passengers and Parcels, between Lancaster and Kendal. to set out every Morning *(Sundays excepted)* at 8 o'clock.

Advertisement for the packet boat service, Kendal Advertiser & Chronicle.
Courtesy Local Studies Section, Kendal Library

Hincaster tunnel.
Courtesy Margaret Duff Collection

whilst lying on their backs. What about the horses? Remarkably, they wandered over the hill by themselves, along a special path, waiting for the barge at the far end of the tunnel. Another impressive structure, also built by Rennie, is the Sedgwick aqueduct. Along the northern reaches of the canal most of the fine Rennie bridges remain to this day.

The Kendal to Lancaster stretch of the canal had cost upwards of £600,000. Opening had been fixed for a date early in May 1819, but this was postponed by the bursting of an embankment about seven miles from Kendal. On June 19th 1819 a local paper reported:

> The Kendal and Lancaster Canal opened for navigation yesterday. All business was suspended, the shops were closed, flags were hoisted, and the bells were rung. A procession of packets from Kendal met a procession from Lancaster at Crooklands, and the combined procession of 16 boats and packets proceeded to Kendal. The proceedings included a dinner at the Town Hall to which 120 sat down. There was a very numerous list of toasts – for instance – the Mayor gave 'A bottle at night and business in the morning.' T. Wilson, Esq. gave 'The Bonny Lasses of Westmorland' and 'Old Wine and Young Women,' and the concluding toast was 'Champagne to our real friends and real pain to our sham friends.'

They seem to have been a feisty lot! A ball in the evening terminated the day's festivities.

Prior to the development of the railways, the canal was also an important means of transport for passengers, and an advertisement of 1802 offered trips between Preston and Lancaster:

For safety, economy and comfort, no other mode of convenience could be eligible, for there the body might be at ease and the most delicate mind without fear.

Which is more than can be said of twenty-first century motorways. From 1820 a daily passenger service plied between Preston and Kendal, taking fourteen hours, tea and refreshments being served on board. In 1833 an express passenger service was introduced, to compete with the stagecoaches, the time being reduced to seven and a half hours. Four galloping horses provided the speed and were changed every four miles. Stables were constructed at intervals for change of horses, and boathouses were also added. Single fare cost 6s first class, and 4s second class. This water journey must have been delightful, passing through such lovely peaceful countryside.

In its heyday the canal would often ring with the sound of children singing and laughing on organised outings such as those of the Kendal Sunday

Schools: they could be heard clearly up in Natland. On these occasions the barges would have been cleaned up and decorated with flags and flowers. Sometimes there would be tea and sports in Levens Park. During a particularly severe winter in the 1920s the canal was frozen for fifteen weeks, and six horses were needed to haul the laden barges over the frozen sections. In the dark of winter the barges carried large lanterns. At night the barges were moored at the various boathouses.

Occasionally the canal sprang a leak through a so-called 'blowhole.' Ernie James, who worked as a bank ranger till 1947, and knew the canal intimately, explained how this happened. The fissured limestone underground caused a great deal of trouble, especially down towards Larkrigg Farm. Air or natural gas filtered into these subterranean galleries, and as the water table rose in time of flood in the River Kent, this was trapped and compressed. The resulting pressure built up till forced to find an outlet. The clay puddle used for lining the canal was easily breached, forming a 'blowhole.' As the water table fell, pressure eased, and the water leaked out through the blowhole into the fissure beneath. It fell to Ernie to block the leak. He made it sound ever so simple, but it must have entailed enormous skill and physical effort.

With the opening of the railways the decline of the canal set in, and in 1855 Parliament dissolved the Canal Corporation, vesting the undertaking in the

Barge from Wigan Coal & Iron Co. Ltd. taking people out on the canal for Sunday School Treat to Levens at the turn of the 20th century.

Courtesy Margaret Duff Collection

Railway Company. Canal traffic dwindled – stone, cement, bricks, lime, clay, coal, in ever-decreasing quantities – till, prior to the Second World War, it was almost non-existent. During the War, however, the canal was once again used for carrying coal from Preston to Kendal, the last load being drawn along in 1947. The canal could have been preserved as a valuable local amenity, for activities such as walking, fishing and boating; but the powers-that-be thought otherwise. The $2\frac{1}{2}$ mile length from Kendal to Crowpark Bridge, and later, in 1957, the rest of the northern section as far south as Stainton, were drained. From Kendal to Crowpark Bridge, and subsequently as far as Larkrigg Hall Bridge, the canal was filled in with Kendal refuse. Soil was spread over the surface and seeded with grass, and the former canal reverted to farmland. A footpath, fenced between Kendal and Crowpark, follows the line of the old towpath. On the 'infilled' section, apart from the footpath and adjoining walls and hedges, as well as the old embankments and cuttings, the old canal is almost indistinguishable from the surrounding fields, appearing much as it must have done before the canal was built. The field boundaries have doubtless been altered in places: I haven't been able to trace a pre-canal map showing the original field pattern.

Between Larkrigg Spring and Sedgwick, and south of Sedgwick, the old canal banks have been bulldozed in, and the ground around levelled off – though fortunately the beautiful bridges have been left. Incidentally, most of the bridges, on the towpath side, have notches, at towrope level, cut over the years by friction as the barges were towed by. Sometimes there are holes where iron bars had been fixed to protect the stone corners. When the canal was emptied, it became marshy in places, and home to water-loving plants such as marsh marigold, water mint, purple loosestrife and meadowsweet. Amongst the plants could be found stranded fresh-water mussels – not bearing pearls like their salt-water relatives! In the wooded section of Larkrigg Spring, trees such as willow, birch and hazel soon took over, as a succession of plants takes over any empty space.

Fishing was always a popular sport on the canal – little boys with their sticks and string as well as fishermen with proper rod and tackle. Occasionally there were charabancs parked on the Green, having brought fishermen from the cities for fishing competitions on the canal. Generations of Natland children must have skated, slid and 'rafted' on the canal, with many a wetting to account for. There have been fatalities too, such as occur wherever there is water.

The canal should never have been closed: as with the railway closures, the powers-that-be didn't look ahead. Many people, however, realised that a considerable asset was being lost. A Restoration Committee was formed, and worked out a scheme for raising money to finance the work. Their proposals seemed entirely practicable. The lovely northern reaches had great 'amenity' value. A restored canal would attract large numbers of walkers, anglers and pleasure boaters, and, as an area of special ecological interest, would have great educational potential for field studies. Financial returns might accrue from the levying of a toll on pleasure craft, mooring fees, and the sale of surplus water to industry. It was proposed to construct a marina, a restaurant and perhaps a swimming pool at the Kendal terminus. It was even suggested that the canal could become an alternative route to the Lake District: a canal route to Windermere had been planned in the past, and might still be feasible. Sadly these ambitious plans were not to materialise, and sometime in the 1960s they were abandoned.

In recent years there has been an upsurge of interest. In spite of the intrusions of the M6, and other 'minor' practical problems, the proposals were revived. The headline '£150M CANAL WILL GO AHEAD' appeared in the *Westmorland Gazette* in 1989; and some time later we read, 'CANAL RE-BIRTH IS NOW IN SIGHT.' In February 2000 we were told that 'The canal is not just a pipe-dream … Trust focuses on 2005 for opening of Kendal section … Leisure facility could bring in millions to the local economy.' Well, so it might: figures of millions are bandied about so blithely these days. We shall have to wait and see. Who knows what effect the proposed restoration of the canal would have on our village?

Dilly Bridge, Natland Road (outskirts of Kendal) – disappeared with road widening in 1968.
Courtesy late Mrs. Maples

The Canal – Late News:
From the *Westmorland Gazette*, February 24th 2006:

> The world-renowned consortium that designed London's winning
> 2012 Olympic bid has been recruited to plan the first phase of the
> ambitious Lancaster Canal restoration … by autumn we should have
> the finer details of how we can take the project to the next level with
> regards to planning and funding to restore the first phase of the
> Northern Reaches of the Lancaster Canal …The key to the project is
> identifying what Kendal needs in terms of commercial and leisure
> facilities while allowing landowners to benefit from the opportunity
> to develop around a high-quality vibrant water space.

Hal Bagot, Chairman of the Lancaster Canal Restoration Partnership, said,
'This is a highly significant event for Kendal, as it is a major leap forward not
only for the restoration of the Lancaster Canal through Kendal, but also in
due course to enable full restoration to the rest of the canal system
throughout England.'

REBELS

Natland's roads have always brought visitors – friends, enemies, gypsies –
even, on one occasion, a royal prince laying claim to the throne on his
father's behalf. The Jacobite rebel army of the '1715' came down from
Scotland through Kendal, commandeering funds and supplies in spite of the
fact that local people tended to support the new Protestant King George I,
formerly Prince George Louis of Hanover. In the autumn of 1745 history
repeated itself when the 'Young Pretender,' Charles Edward, led his rebel
army into England. At Penrith on November 20th he heard his father
proclaimed King James III. The Jacobite rebels stayed only one night in
Kendal – the proclamation being solemnly read out once more in the Market
Place. Almost certainly the rebels passed through Natland. Country people,
terrified by the rebel army, hastily hid away their valuables. After the
disastrous battle of Derby, the rebels set off north in disarray. They reached
Kendal on Saturday, December 13th, in vile weather conditions. It
happened to be Market Day and the town was thronged. Alderman Shaw
took the initiative and, mounted on his horse, rallied the stallholders to pelt
the defeated rebels with whatever came to hand. When the Scots began to
fight back Shaw had to escape on horseback up Entry Lane. The skirmish
developed, moving to Finkle Street, the road to Scotland; halfway down the
street firing broke out and four people were killed. Their deaths are in the
Parish Registers:

Dec. 15th – Richard Toulman of Highgate, killed by ye Rebbals.
"   – Archibald Armstronge of Highgate   ditto

"   – John Slack of New Hutton killed by ye Scots.
"   – Scotch reball his name not known.

Meanwhile, Prince Charles was being entertained by Mr Justice Shepherd at his home, 95 Stricklandgate. The Prince stayed there only one night, joining his army as they fled north, as fast as dreadful road conditions allowed. They had so many carriages and wheeled wagons that they were forced to halt about four miles north of Kendal at Forest Hall. At Clifton they were met and attacked by the Duke of Cumberland, this being the last battle on English soil. The Prince escaped, but many of his company were killed and buried at Clifton. The Jacobites were finally annihilated by Cumberland, with dreadful slaughter, at Culloden. The Duke of Cumberland's reputation for ruthlessness earned him the nickname 'Butcher Cumberland,' but Kendal people evidently saw him differently: he is remembered today in the name of the Duke of Cumberland Inn. Today 95 Stricklandgate, always known as Prince Charlie's House, houses 'Charlie's Bar.'

There is an interesting description of the Prince's appearance in the diary of a young Manchester woman, Elizabeth Byrom (quoted in J.J. Bagley, *Historical Interpretation*, 2 vols [Newton Abbot: David and Charles,1972], 2, p. 93). On November 27th, when the rebel army was approaching the town, she wrote:

> The postmaster is gone to London today, we suppose to secure the money from falling into the hands of the rebels; we expect a party of them here tomorrow. The Prince lay at Lawyer Starkey's at Preston last night; he has marched from Carlisle on foot at the head of his army; he was dressed in a Scotch plaid, a blue silk waistcoat with silver lace, and a Scotch bonnet with J.R. on it. Yesterday the militia were all discharged and went home, but just in time before the Highlanders came – well contrived.

Perhaps even today there is still some lingering Jacobite sympathy in Scotland. I myself have seen an old carving, on a stone in a remote valley in northern Scotland, of the Jacobite symbol of a wineglass.

Chapter 6

OCCUPATIONS

THE POST OFFICE AND VILLAGE SHOP

In 1897 Thomas Huck was running a postal service from 'Town End;' later this service was run from 7 Church View (now demolished), but what the service entailed can only be guessed. Since 1922 the Post Office has been located in the village shop; according to Post Office records, Mrs Shepherd, who ran the shop from soon after the First World War, was Postmistress till 1932, when her daughter took over from her. According to a Directory of 1930, deliveries were made at 7.50 am with despatches at 9.40 am and 5.20 pm. Deliveries were made on foot from Kendal at first, and later by bicycle. Motorised delivery started in 1947, and the little red Post Office vans became a familiar sight. In the late 60s we got our post about breakfast time. Officially those living on the afternoon collection route would have a second delivery. In earlier days there had been a 1d post, but the price rose gradually, till about 1960 1st class mail was 5d, 2nd class 4d. In recent years, of course, many rural Post Offices have been closed down: when Sedgwick Post Office closed a few years ago, the village shop disappeared with it. The Sedgwick telephone exchange, which served Natland, was operated manually till 1948. The nearest telegraph office was at Sedgwick

Earliest photograph showing Natland PO (previously an inn) with stables to left.
Note the door on upper floor where cock fighting took place!

Courtesy Graham Needham

79

PO in 1990s with Mary Carruther's little Jack Russell dog 'Lucy' outside –
she was a real character and everybody knew her.

Courtesy Graham Needham

Graham and Liz Needham outside the PO in June 2006.

PO, though up till the late 60s telegrams could be handed in at Oxenholme Station.

Mrs Shepherd built up a thriving business. Every Thursday she made 28 pounds of 'haver' bread on an old-fashioned backstone, using all her shop refuse such as boxes and cartons for fuel – thrift indeed! This 'haver' was well known. Mrs Shepherd always wore a lace cap, which intrigued me as a small child when I was taken to buy sweets whilst on holiday at Natland Abbey. Her daughter ran the shop and Post Office till 1944. From then we had a succession of shopkeepers-Postmasters – Mr Holden; Mr Wynne (who changed the half-day closing from Wednesday to Saturday); Mr Broadbent; Mr Haworth; Mr Bradby; Mr Howes; and the present occupier, Mr Graham Needham. All, needless to say, were ably supported by their wives. Mrs Broadbent lived in the village till very recently, dying at the grand old age of 99 on March 27th 2006. The shop and Post Office have been kept as a cheerful centre of village life. The *Westmorland Gazette* of May 1st 1998 featured an article on Rural Development, with emphasis on the need to support village shops and Post Offices: 'use them or lose them.' Graham Needham and his staff have always aimed to please their customers – unfailingly cheerful and helpful, with a friendly word for everyone. In the shop one meets people, one chats and gets the latest news. The village notice board, on the front wall of the shop, always makes interesting reading. One person, visiting from Canada, had especially enjoyed the bacon and cheese from Graham's shop, and decided he would take some back home, sneaking the package through Customs in his luggage: good for him!

FARMING

In 1919 there were twelve farms scattered round Natland, and the parish included land belonging to Oxenholme Farm. Since then several of the Natland farms have ceased to operate as such, and have become private dwellings, their lands being sold or let to other farms, as small acreages became uneconomical to run. One of the 'lost' farms is Crowpark, which was bought by the Hudson family, who bred whippets. Greenside Farm, formerly known as Hollad or Halhead (I think it was Mr Jack Howson who changed the name about the end of the 1920s), became a private dwelling. Higher House was bought by the Croft family in 1946, though the land continued to be farmed by its former occupant, Mr Bob Bindloss. Mr Croft owned an agricultural implements business in Kendal, and used the big barn as a store; the barn was demolished long ago after the roof fell in. Lower House Farm also became a private dwelling when Mr Atkinson Moorhouse retired: he built a bungalow, Sundown, close by, and, as we have seen, converted one of his barns into two cottages. Mr and Mrs Bindloss

Aerial View showing clear layout of village in 1960s. Note the former farms – Greenside and Town End Farm.

Aerofilms & Aero Pictorial Ltd.

Courtesy Margaret Duff Collection

moved into one of them, now called Bield. Natland Abbey's farm buildings were demolished in 1962 when the Abbey Drive development started. Town End is also no longer a farm. Some time about the end of the First World War it was worked as a combined smithy and farm by Mr Jack Dixon (the smithy had earlier been on the Green, and was rebuilt as 6 and 7 Church View). The Town End farm buildings and land were later let off. There was no longer a resident blacksmith, but for some years the smithy was used by Mr Mitchell from Crosthwaite. The horse-shoeing trade died as the farm horses disappeared. Mr Mitchell did a considerable amount of wrought iron work, making handsome gates for many Natland houses. I was told that the old house was formerly called The Laurels, and before that, Smithy Farm; it has now reverted to its original name, Town End. Watercrook Farm, built on part of the site of the ancient Roman camp, Alauna, was sold to K Shoes,

Milk kits at Natland Hall awaiting collection by Libby's from Milnthorpe.
This is one of the stands where local farmers left their milk.
NB. Park cottages opposite.

who built a large storage depot on the field known as Chamber Ings. For a time the house and land were let off.

Natland Parish consists of good fertile land supporting mixed farming – meadow, arable, dairy stock, fat stock and sheep. In past times oats, wheat, kale, potatoes, turnips and mangolds were the general crops. A snapshot: in 1932 the parish contained 208 milking cows, 177 beef cattle, 680 sheep, 37 horses and some pigs. Some of the milk was delivered round the village (the farmers each had their milk round), and much of the rest was sent to Libby's in Milnthorpe.

Last year, 2005, there were many acres of Indian corn or maize: is this a reflection of changing weather patterns, or merely changing farming fashion? Shorthorn cattle were widely kept during the 1920s and 30s, and were superseded by the black and white Friesians: Natland Park Farm exported their Friesians to many parts of the world. There were also a few Ayrshires, with an occasional Jersey cow. Fat stock rearing has become increasingly widespead – white-headed red Herefords, black Galloways and Charolais with their curly cream coats. I am told that nowadays the sheep bred here are mostly Half-bred Mules, which are a cross between a Teeswater tup and a Rough ewe; the brown-faced Suffolk sheep are also kept. Most farmers keep poultry of one sort or another.

The making of silage has been a development of the last few decades, which has been an advantage in our climate: hay-making needs sunshine. The devastating outbreak of foot and mouth disease in 2001 fortunately did not affect Natland directly. In general, though, farmers in our region, particularly the hill farmers, are having a tough time.

OTHER OCCUPATIONS

It is possible that at one time some Natlanders worked as charcoal burners. Definite evidence that charcoal burning was carried out is to be found in the old coppice woodland of Larkrigg Spring. The most important feature is a pitstead: this is a flattened circular platform, formed by digging into sloping ground. On the pitstead lengths of wood were built into a beehive shape; this was in turn covered with straw, then a layer of sand or earth to slow down the burning process. The structure was lit from the centre. Great care had to be taken to prevent rapid burning, which would consume the wood completely. The whole process took several days, and six loads of wood were needed to produce one load of charcoal. In the Spring there are also traces of one or two huts in which the charcoal burners would sleep. The charcoal was used in the local iron smelting industry. (On charcoal burning, see William Rollinson, *A History of Man in the Lake District*, [London: Dent, 1967], pp. 108-9.)

A considerable number of Natland men were employed at the Gunpowder Works at Sedgwick. These had been started by the Wakefield family in 1764, and were eventually absorbed by Imperial Chemical Industries in 1917. The Natland men walked to work there through the fields by Larkrigg Hall Bridge, crossing the river Kent by the footbridge near the works. Old Mr Sill told me that his father worked there on three shifts, 6 am-2 pm, 2 pm-10 pm, and 10 pm. to 6 am, working through a long weekend every fortnight – for £1 a week! Others were not so lucky to get that extra time in. Life must have been difficult on that money, with a growing family to maintain. Mr Sill retired about the time the works closed down in 1935.

Many of the local men were employed at the expanding K Shoe works in Kendal. Several Oxenholme people worked at the paper mill at Burneside, travelling to work on the morning mail train at 6 am, and returning on the 4 pm. There was a considerable demand for domestic servants, gardeners and handymen in the bigger houses. These were mostly built in the Victorian era – Ross Lodge, Newlands, Oxenholme House, Helme Bank, High Park, and Uphill (later Windy Brow and Grassgarth). Other large houses, High Wells, Fisherflatt, Elstead and Brough Fold were built before the First World War. All needed domestic staff. In 1919 Mrs Gibson was still running her laundry at Laundry Cottage, now Compton House: her clientèle included the big houses, and many villagers sent their menfolk's Sunday collars to be stiffly starched. I couldn't trace when the laundry closed down. There have been various small shops in Natland and up at Oxenholme. In the Directory of 1930 Mr E. Langhorne is listed as a boot maker and repairer at Helmside, and he was still there when my family moved to Natland.

There were two grocers at Bolefoot, Mr Parker and Mrs Swainbank. For about twenty years the Kendal Cooperative Society had a branch at Oxenholme, which closed in the 1960s. There was also a butcher's shop too at one time, doubling as a confectioner's and newsagent's. Reuben Swainbank was a haulage contractor at Helmside. Mr Sam Ingram was a joiner, painter and paperhanger. Up at the Station Inn the licensee was J.C. Dixon. Mr Joe Wood retired in the late 1960s from his filling station, shop and taxi business at the south end of Oxenholme, which he had run from 1945, and Mr Powley took over. These businessmen were also assisted by their wives.

At some forgotten date there was a little sweet shop at 1 Church View (back in Natland), though I have also been told that this was a cobbler's shop. Mr Dick Holmes had a greengrocery business in this house when we came to live in Natland in 1948. It was in 1938 that Dick Holmes started the family-owned business of R. Holmes and Sons, nurserymen and florists, in the village, and several members of the family are still involved in the business.

Oxenholme Co-operative.
Courtesy late Mrs. Maples

Mr and Mrs. Woods, Oxenholme Garage.

Courtesy late Mrs. Maples

Holmes Nursery celebrating their 50th anniversary in 1988.
Front row: Lyn, Brian, Ronnie and Roger Holmes. Back row l to r: Stephen Holmes,
Keith McDougall, Mark Shepherd, Ruth Holmes and Ronald Holmes.

Westmorland Gazette   *Courtesy Local Studies Section, Kendal Library*

They have needed to extend their premises from time to time, and to provide adequate parking. Two of Dick's sons, Ronnie and Brian, joined their Dad, and eventually also the grandsons. The third son, George, built up his building and joinery business, with a workshop in the barn opposite Lower House; very sadly, George died recently and is greatly missed as he did so much for Natland. The youngest son, John, worked as a panel-beater and was an expert in restoring cars that had come to grief. The nursery is well known: in fact, when Natland is mentioned quite far afield, the response is 'Oh yes, that's where Holmes's gardens are.' May they long continue.

Mr. D. Trotter, Fruit & Veg, Oxenholme.
Courtesy late Mrs. Maples

Mr. R. R. Holmes.
Courtesy late Mrs. Maples

Mr Trotter had a travelling greengrocery van for many years, and this was carried on by one of his sons, who dealt in fish as well. The Trotter family lived quite near Oxenholme Garage. For many years greengrocer's, fishmonger's and butcher's vans were a feature of village life; the Endmoor and District Cooperative Society had a traveller, Mr Hallion, who took orders, and groceries were delivered to the door.

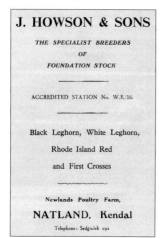

Several other kinds of business have been built up in the village, some still with us today. The Poultry Farm at Newlands was taken over by Mr Jim Howson in 1937. With the help of his two sons, Sid and Edwin, he bred day-old chicks and laying stock: very much a specialised market. They raised about 100,000 chicks a year, starting hatching at Christmas time. Eventually Sid took over, later installing hen batteries – at that time quite a new development in poultry keeping.

Advertisement in Flower Show programme 1955.
Courtesy late Mrs. Maples

88

Mr. W. Barnes, Hardware Merchant, Oxenholme.

Courtesy late Mrs. Maples

Jim Frearson, a wood craftsman, worked from his home at Boundary Cottage, and later Overdale near Helmside. He rented a stretch of the mosses at Witherslack, cutting, drying and burning his peat for home fuel – a pointer, perhaps, for future years if our present supplies of fuel run out. Mr Bill Moffat of Hawes Lane, now retired, was an agricultural contractor, having taken over the business started many years ago by his father. He was kept very busy all through the farming year, working with those huge machines that have eased the hardest work on local farms. There were several builders: Arthur Brown, who lived in the village, Charnley, Purvis and Newby, and Ingram and Lambert. In 1959 Miss Cleland brought her Birkfell Kennels (Boarding and Breeding) to Natland, down at Hawes Bank, near Crowpark Bridge on the way down to the river. Her white West Highland Terriers won international repute and were exported as far afield as Canada, the USA and Sweden. More than half of her breeding stock were champions, and I think it was in 1969 that one of her dogs gained the distinction of 'Best of Breed' at Crufts. The different kinds of employment pursued by Natland's present-day inhabitants would require a lengthy list, as would the former occupations of numerous retired people. In living memory at least, unemployment has never been a serious problem in Natland.

Advertisement in Flower Show programme 1955.

Courtesy late Mrs. Maples

*John Atkinson
with his two
grandchildren Ben and
Neil Allen.*
*Courtesy
John Atkinson*

*Mike and Barbara
Nelson.*
*Courtesy
Barbara Nelson*

Three Mayors of Kendal

In the 1980s and 90s no fewer than three Mayors of Kendal were residents of Natland and Oxenholme, which was quite an honour for the village. John Atkinson was Mayor from 1983-84, Mike Nelson from 1987-88, and Philip Ball from 1995-96, 1996-97 and 1997-98. Philip Ball's three successive terms of office were something of a record.

Westmorland Gazette Reporters

It seems we have always had a reporter of village affairs for the *Westmorland Gazette*. Ingrid Beattie took over from Sam Inglesfield in the late 1980s, and Rhian Peters in turn took over in 2003. In earlier years William Cartmell reported on Natland developments. This is an important service, and their weekly reports are always interesting and informative.

A Guardian of the Lakes

One distinguished resident of Natland was Kenneth Himsworth, who lived at Cracalt House with his wife Ethelburga and family; when elderly, he went to live in Chester near his daughter. Kenneth was for many years Clerk to Westmorland County Council and the Lake District Joint Planning Board. He was a great defender of the Lake District National Park. He died in 2005.

Jennifer and Philip Ball.

Courtesy Philip Ball

Old Church demolished in 1909.

J. Simcoe

Courtesy John Marsh Collection

Interior of old church – note the oil lamps.

Courtesy John Marsh Collection

Chapter 7

THE CHURCH

THE TITHES

Natland was originally a chapelry within the large parish of Kendal Holy Trinity, which was the Mother Church. In 1246 'Ralph Daincurt gave to Master Roger Pepin, rector of the mediety of the church at Kirkebi in Kendale, land in Natalunt in a competent place, 80 ft in length and 40 in breadth, to hold during his life, for the site of a barn in which to put his tithe of Natalunt' (see above, 'Records of the Barony of Kendale'). The tithe barn stood across the lane from the south-west corner of the present churchyard. In the 1950s a bungalow named 'Tithe Barn' was built on the site of the ancient barn, and during construction old foundations, perhaps belonging to the original structure of 1246, were revealed. Natland was in the Archdeaconry of Richmond, which until 1541 was part of the Diocese of York. As we have seen, it is probable that Natland Abbey was used by St Mary's Abbey, York to collect tithes and rents. In 1541 the southern part of what is now the Diocese of Carlisle was transferred to the Bishopric of Chester, and it was not until the 1850s that the diocese took its present shape. After the Dissolution of the monasteries in the mid-sixteenth century, the Rectory of Kendal passed from St. Mary's Convent at York to the Crown. In 1553 Queen Mary bestowed it to Trinity College, Cambridge. The tithes were originally paid in kind. Eventually, in 1834, in order to settle the many disputes that the tithe system caused, the Kendal Corn Rent Act was passed, laying down definite sums based on the price of crops: these rents were apportioned among the Chapelries of Kendal Parish Church. The total amount of Corn Rent for Natland was £112. The Kendal Corn Rent Bill of 1932 enabled individual tithe-payers to redeem their tithe at any time.

CHURCH BUILDINGS

Life in most villages revolves round the Church and village School. It was only as recently as 1872 that Natland became a parish in its own right. Records are vague and scanty, but one thing is certain – there has been a Chapel or Church here for many centuries. In a document of 1312 there is a reference to 'the cross in Nateland:' this cross, of stone or wood, presumably stood on the Green, and was doubtless used by itinerant preaching friars. Parts of an Anglian cross were found during alterations at Kendal Parish Church. In 1246 'Roger Pepyn, parson of the mediety of the church in Kyrkeby in Kendale' granted that Ralph de Eyncurt and his heirs 'should henceforth have a chapel in their court at Natelund for the celebration of divine service' (see above, 'Records of the Barony of Kendale'). This must refer to Natland Hall, though we don't know whether the chapel was an integral part of the Hall itself or a separate building. As we have seen, when Thomas Machell visited here in 1691 there was 'a little chapel lately rebuilt.' During the next two centuries there was throughout the country a very considerable amount of church building and restoration. Natland Church formerly held lands at Skelsmergh, Old Hutton and Barbon; similarly, within Natland Parish there were pieces of land belonging to other parishes. There were several charities. Still hanging in the present church is this notice:

> Donation for Bread –1842.
> John Creighton of Natland, left 19 guineas,
> the interest thereof to be given in bread, to poor
> householders attending divine service in this church.

John Creighton lived and farmed at Cracalt; his charity was administered by the Vicar and Churchwardens. The Charles Shippard Charity goes back to about 1779, and was for the general benefit of 'Poor Persons.' The income of less than £5 per year was from certain lands in Natland, including land farmed by Natland Hall. The Trustees were self-appointing, meeting once a year in time to make some distribution before Christmas. Both charities are today held in abeyance.

The list of incumbents hangs in the Church porch:

1735 – Thomas Head
1738 – William Wade
1741 – James Godmond
1747 – William Towson
1777 – George Kendal
1804 – Thomas Briggs M.A.
1816 – Thomas Thornbarrow
1818 – John Corry (Curate)
1819 – Thomas Mackereth
1825 – Joseph Fawcett
1828 – Ralph. W. Fisher (Curate)
1830 – John Sampson B.A. (Curate)
1861 – Frederick T. Salmon (Curate)
1863 – Isaac Bowman (Curate)
1865 – James Inglis (Curate)
1866 – Edward Bannerman
1871 – James I. Duncan.
1875 – Charles Whitaker B.A.
1897 – William Kewley
1907 – Edward J. Miller M.A.

1950 – Donald E. Marrs A.L.C.D.
1957 – George E. Jenkins M.A.
1962 – Eric Mann
1970 – R. Michael L.Westropp M.A.
1975 – Colin P. Stannard T.D., M.A.
1984 – Trevor Park B.A., S.Tn.
1997 – Tim Evans M.A.

In Natland two new Churches were built in 1735 and 1825. The profits of two enclosures belonging to the township, together with an annual subscription, were given by the inhabitants to a person who should teach their children and read prayers in the chapel on Sundays. Further money was obtained later from Queen Anne's Bounty and other sources, so that in 1777 the revenue amounted to about £33 a year. The Church building of 1735 had a small churchyard, not used for burials. Its site was apparently about a hundred yards from the present Church, and about ten yards from the 'pot house' – presumably the Horse and Farrier Inn (now the village shop). Almost certainly this Church stood on the site of the former Chapel, where Compton House now stands. Both Mrs Cook, who lived in part of the house, and Mrs Pooley Nelson confirmed that this was the site of the Chapel. When trenches were dug for the sewerage scheme, incidentally, some regular stonework was exposed a few yards from the Post Office, on the opposite side of the road from Compton House. A map of 1770 marked the Church as being right in the centre of the Green, and Cracalt and Crowpark appear to have changed places: such early maps are notoriously inaccurate. Curiously, there used to be two old yew trees just over the wall from Lower House, opposite the present Vicarage. Old Mr Sill told me that there used to be an old barn-like building there, which had been burnt down when he was a boy. Old yew trees are often associated with the former presence of a church. Could the barn have been the remains of yet another church or chapel, unrecorded?

By the early 1820s an increase in population brought the need for a larger Church. The new site was a hundred yards from the old one – the site, in fact, of the present Church. The first stone was laid on 29 November 1823 (*Records*, 3, p. 114). At last Natland had its own burial ground: until this time burials took place at Kendal. The earliest register for Natland Church is dated 1777: as we have seen, before this date baptisms, marriages and funerals were recorded in the registers of Kendal Parish Church. Thomas Head was Vicar of this third church – the cost of which was £550, of which £100 was given by the Society for the Building of New Churches, and the rest subscribed by parishioners – £300 of it by three individuals. According to the custom of the time the pews were numbered, with most reserved for particular persons or for the occupants of the bigger houses, and the rest

Laying foundation stone of new Church. Mr. James Howie, builder, adjusts the stone. Canon Trench stands with Col. Crewdson. Robert Washington Halhead (descendent of the De Wessingtons) builder's foreman, directs D. Howie and workmen at the winch. Higginson, the Gazette reporter (r. of left-hand scaffold pole) scribbles in his notebook. John Howson and Tom Goodwin, the schoolmaster's son who trained as a teacher and died young, turn round. Miss Proctor's hat is the middle of three, her sister's right.

Gilbert Hogg

Courtesy Margaret Duff Collection

being set apart for the 'poor inhabitants'! The chancel was very small, and the pulpit and reading desk were placed about half way down the south side, with the pews facing them. This was changed in 1872 when the church was re-seated at a cost of £350. In 1879 a new chancel, organ and vestry were built, the communion table, rails and tablets were removed and replaced, and the pulpit and reading desk moved to the north and south sides of the chancel.

The Railway Company provided a Reading Room at Helmside, and a Railway Children's Choir helped to raise the £850 needed to build the Oxenholme Railway Mission, close to the railway bridge, which was opened in 1906: the building still stands. Services in the Mission Hall were conducted by Mrs Page of Brough Fold and Mr Parker of Helm Mount, Oxenholme, and several Natland people apparently attended. Mrs Page called her children's class her 'Busy Bees.' Concerts, dances, talks and children's parties all took place in the Railway Mission.

The various alterations made to the existing Natland Church proved inadequate; more particularly, with the increase in population resulting from the building of railway houses at Helmside and Oxenholme in the 1880s and 90s, the building was simply too small. In 1908 Austin and Paley of Lancaster, well known architects of the period, were called in to advise on whether to extend the Church. This they considered a waste of money: there were too many structural faults, and so on. It was decided to pull down the Church and rebuild. Austin and Paley designed the new Church in the Late Decorated style, and it was built by Messrs. Howie and Sons of Kendal, at a cost in the region of £5905 (you could hardly get a kitchen fitted for this price today). Much of this cost was met by the Crewdson family.

During the twenty-seven months of building, permission was granted for services to be held in the School, and a barn at Cracalt was used for the administration of the Sacraments. The foundation stone of the new St Mark's Church was laid in June 1909, and the building was consecrated on November 7th 1910. The Lancaster stone came by canal barge to Crowpark Bridge, and the Darley Dale stone for dressings came by train and was fashioned on the spot. The font was carved *in situ* from one solid block of stone. The pillar between the font and the south door is said to have the largest circumference of any in an English parish church. Nikolaus Pevsner, in his Buildings of England volume, *Cumberland and Westmorland* (Harmondsworth: Penguin, 1967), quotes Temple Moore's remark that Natland Church is 'as good as any of the churches by the best church architects of those years,' adding, 'It is a resourceful and strong interior, not at all mannered or pedantic' (p. 280).

The first Vicarage.

Courtesy Canon Tim Evans

The present Vicarage, built in 1803.

Courtesy Canon Tim Evans

The Church contains beautiful stained glass, all of it post-Second World War, with the exception of the Crewdson window in the baptistery, which was installed in 1912 in memory of Katharine Crewdson, and the 1938 window in memory of Keith Aidan Sinker, in the side chapel of the south aisle. The Keesey window of 1946 was given by Mrs Keesey of Fisherflatt, who lost her husband in the First World War and her son in the Second. The fine east window, also of 1946, commemorates Ernest Mark Cecil Maples, who was also killed in the Second World War: like the Sinker window this was designed by Gerald E. R. Smith, and as in the earlier window rainbows are incorporated in its design. The Millennium window, installed in 2000, was designed and made by local stained glass artist Sarah Walkley, and was given by Kenneth Wilkinson in memory of his wife Lilian. The Church also contains several brass memorial plaques: a plaque in the side chapel replaced two stained glass memorial windows in the old Church. In 1948 nine names were added to the War Memorial: G.W. Armer, E.S. Ferguson, J.M. Fothergill, J. Hudson, W.J. Howson, A.R. Hodgson, J.H. Keesey, H. King and E.M.C. Maples. 128 young people from Natland and Oxenholme, including 13 women, had served in the Forces during the Second World War.

When it was first built, the present Church, like the School, was lit by acetylene gas – no doubt considered very up-to-date at that time; the 'gas house' consisted of a shed at the top of the school playground. Mr and Mrs Hodgson were the caretakers: their duties included looking after the lighting system, cleaning the church, laundering the church linen, keeping the churchyard tidy, and ringing the church bell, for which they were paid quarterly, 10s a week. They carried out these duties for fifteen years, up to about 1929. When Natland acquired mains electricity in 1935, electric lighting was installed in the Church; in 1947 the organ was modernised with the installation of an electric blower. In the late 1970s it was decided to build an extension, providing a clergy vestry, a utility room for the preparation of light refreshments, and toilet facilities. The existing clergy and choir vestries were converted into one large room, to serve both as a choir vestry and a meeting place to accommodate 40-50 people. The cost of the work was £18,500, much of which was given by parishioners or raised by parish events. The extension was dedicated by the Bishop of Carlisle on October 9th 1981. At present the churchyard, which was extended in 1926, is nearing full capacity: the small space needed for the interment of ashes will have to be taken into account.

THE VICARAGE

At some time during his incumbency (1825-28), Joseph Fawcett, the 'perpetual curate' of Natland, wrote to Mr W. D. Crewdson:

Mothers' Union Sale of Work in Vicarage garden in the 1950s. Colonel Crewdson front left and Rev. Marrs and Mrs. Marrs (sitting down, wearing striped suit).
Pictured above –
Colonel Crewdson.

Miss Proctor is pictured in the middle leaning across, wearing a felt hat, at the bric-a-brac stall.
Courtesy Philip Ball

Having no parsonage, I have hitherto rented a house of W.W.C. Wilson, Esq., of Casterton Hall (who has considerable property in the Chapelry) at the annual rent of £9 – which low rent was fixed by the owner, with a view to inducing the Minister to reside. The said House is about 100 yards from the Chapel, is now in good repair, sufficiently large for a considerable Family, has a good Garden, with a Barn and Stable and other appurtenances, and is in every respect a suitable and desirable residence for the Minister of the Chapel.

Fawcett went on to advise that, since Wilson was now willing to sell the house on very generous terms, it should be bought to provide the 'Minister' with a permanent residence. The house, which stood within what is now the Vicarage garden, to the right of the existing gate, became the first Natland Vicarage. The foundation stone of the present Vicarage was laid on June 25th 1883, as the *Westmorland Gazette* reported:

The new parsonage at Natland is making rapid progress in the hands of the builders, Messrs. Freeman of Stainton. On Monday a memorial stone was laid near the front doorway by Mrs Whitaker, wife of the incumbent. The sealed bottle, which was placed in the hollow of the stone, contained some coins, English and foreign, the latest copy of the *Westmorland Gazette*, a photograph of the school children and St. Mark's Home boys and a copy of the circular issued by Archdeacon Cooper on behalf of the new Parsonage Fund which amounts to £1,000 towards a total estimated cost of £1,300 including the site.

According to the accounts, the total cost was £1,400 of which £700 came from the Diocesan Extension Society, Queen Anne's Bounty and Marshall's Charity, with the remainder from subscriptions.

REV. CHARLES WHITAKER AND ST. MARK'S HOME

One outstanding Vicar of Natland was Charles Whitaker, here from 1875 to 1897. His father, James Whitaker, had been Master of the Blue Coat School in Kendal, and Charles was evidently brought up to have a strong social conscience. He was trained at the London College of Divinity, subsequently working for three years at the St. Peter's, Limehouse Mission. There he saw the pitiful state of the orphan boys in the streets of London; he also met Edward Rudolph, founder of the Waifs and Strays Society, which was later to become the Church of England Children's Society. It was Charles Whitaker's friendship with Rudolph that led to the foundation of St. Mark's Home in Natland. The new School House on the Green provided a temporary home for the first group of 'waifs and strays,' four boys from the streets of London, who arrived in 1882 (when we lived in the School House there were still, in the landing cupboard, labels with the boys' names written on them, pasted next to the clothes hooks). To these city boys the quiet countryside must at first have seemed strange and unfamiliar. In one of a series of articles on local villages, a *Westmorland Gazette* reporter described a visit to the Home:

> Expressing a wish to see the extemporised home, we went there. Half a dozen ruddy, bright little fellows came into the room, saluting as they did so, and then formed into a line. There was something about them different from any other boys connected with an 'Institution' I had ever seen. I can only express what I mean by saying they were out and out boys. Then we had some conversation – full of fun and laughter. They told me their names; their sad reminiscences of town life; and how happy they were here in the pleasant countryside. One would like to be a teacher, another a farmer, a third a soldier, and so on. We were in their library and kind friends had sent them piles of interesting books. Two things struck me – the more than earnestness of the founder of the Home, and the real happiness that beamed upon the boys' faces. St. Mark's Home cannot be otherwise than successful. Each boy has his own particular 'mother' in some lady of the county. She selects her boy and volunteers to clothe and care for him during his stay. Those interested should go themselves and personally see the lads.

St. Mark's Home, Natland in the early 1900s.

Courtesy John Marsh Collection

Mr Whitaker spent a great deal of time stimulating interest and raising money for a bigger building. St. Mark's Home was opened in 1885. Mr Whitaker had several resident students who were preparing to train for the ministry, and he coached at least one bright local boy in Latin and Greek before School in the morning. He was also quite a distinguished theological scholar, publishing several books. *A Sketch of Rufinus and His Time: With his Commentary on the Apostles' Creed and a Translation of the Same*, on the fourth-century theologian Tyrannius Rufinus, was published in Natland in 1887, and apparently printed with the help of St. Mark's Home boys; a 'third edition' of the translation, *Commentary of Rufinus on the Apostle's Creed*, was published in London by George Bell and Sons in 1908. Whitaker's *Students' Aid to the Prayer Book*, intended to help students taking the University Preliminary Theological Examinations, was published by George Bell in 1893. More surprisingly, an essay by Charles Whitaker appeared in a relatively recent volume of essays published in 1978.

In 1947 the Waifs and Strays Society became the Church of England Children's Society. St. Mark's Home became gradually more relaxed, and uniform was abandoned. The Master and Matron, Mr and Mrs Lowe, served there for many years; Mr Lowe died suddenly in 1960. The Home boys played a considerable part in village and Church life, attending the village School, and some joining the Church choir. It is difficult to find out how

Dr. Barnardo's Home, Barrows Green.

Courtesy late Mrs. Maples

they got on in later life. I know of only two who stayed in this area, Danny Child and Paul Slater, both of whom have made good lives for themselves. After Mr Lowe's death the Home was temporarily closed for alterations to the building, reopening in 1961 as a 'family home,' taking both boys and girls. Children's Society policy moved away from residential homes, placing more emphasis on adoptions and care of the handicapped and disturbed teenagers. In April 1975 St Mark's became a 'holiday home,' providing children with special needs with the experience of life in the country. Later there was yet another change of use: renamed 'Appletree School,' the former Home now provided care for boys in need of help. Charles Whitaker would have approved.

For many years there was another children's home just within the Natland parish bounds. Barnardo's Home started at Barrows Green House in 1947, with Mr and Mrs Clarke as Master and Matron; two years later Mr and Mrs Savage took over. The children from Barnardo's attended Crosscrake School before proceeding to secondary education in Kendal. The Home subsequently closed, and the house passed into private use.

SOME NATLAND VICARS OF THE LAST HUNDRED YEARS

The long incumbency of the Rev., later Canon, Edward Miller, from 1907 to 1949, saw many changes. Three years after his arrival the new Church was consecrated. During the later part of the First World War, from October 1917, the Rev. Miller served as an Army Chaplain at the War Hospitals at Gosforth and Sunderland, returning to Natland in early 1919. During his absence a rota of lay readers and fellow clergy attended to the spiritual needs of the parish. In 1919 there were seven baptisms, five weddings and one funeral. In 1920 the Parochial Church Council was brought into being under the Enabling Act. Canon Miller was created a Canon of Carlisle Cathedral in 1935. After his retirement he lived at Spence House, which he had built, with his daughter Eleanor, until his death in 1956. Miss Miller, who taught Religious Studies at Kendal High School, later moved into a converted cottage on Church View.

The Rev. Jenkins stayed at Natland for only four years before retiring. His wife was a very accomplished pianist, and, when we lived in the School House we could hear her practising when the Vicarage sitting room windows were open. The Rev. Eric Mann, who arrived in 1962, was involved in the building of the new School. Canon Trevor Park had a varied and interesting life before he came to Natland from Dalton-in-Furness in 1984. Before ordination he spent two years travelling the world in the Norwegian Merchant Navy; he then served for five years in the Royal Air Force as a Russian linguist, and lived for two years in Norway, where he taught in a

Folk High School; his wife, Olaug is Norwegian. From 1975 he was an elected member of the General Synod, representing the clergy of the Diocese; he also represented the Diocese on the Central Board of Finance of the Church of England, and served on its Publishing Committee. Trevor was co-author of one of the Schools Council 'Journeys into Religion' workbooks, for use in secondary schools, published in 1978, and in 1981 he published a history of St Bees College. Whilst at Natland he was researching into the origins of the early theological colleges of the Church of England. In 2005 Trevor received the MBE for service to the Commonwealth community in Norway and to United Kingdom-Norwegian relations. The present Vicar is Canon Tim Evans, who is assisted by his Curate, Martin Dew, and by non-stipendary Curate Martin Jayne.

Church-Related Organisations

There are various thriving organisations connected with the Church. The Mothers' Union meets in the Vestry on the fourth Tuesday afternoon of the month, from September to May inclusive, with speakers alternating between the serious and the more light-hearted. At present there are twelve members, with Mrs Rena Blight as Branch Leader. The Mothers' Union Families Group is run by Elizabeth Chandler. There are also the Young Wives and the St. Mark's Fellowship associations; Canon Evans runs a Youth Group, and Colleen Harrison is the Coordinator of the Sunday Club. Recently there have been a Parish Visit to Carlisle Cathedral, a Shrove Tuesday Supper and Quiz, Lent lunches, a visit of the Lancaster Music Department Chamber Choir and so on.

Several other religious denominations are, of course, represented in Natland besides the Church of England: Methodist, United Reformed, Roman Catholic, Jehovah's Witness, and no doubt others – not forgetting those individuals who simply draw their inspiration from the surrounding countryside, with all its natural wonders.

School before it was extended with old Church.

Westmorland Gazette.　　　　　　　　　　　*Courtesy Local Studies Section, Kendal Library*

Extension to School and new Church.

Westmorland Gazette.　　　　　　　　　　　*Courtesy Local Studies Section, Kendal Library*

Chapter 8

EDUCATION

Richard Frankland and the Northern Academy

In 1691 Thomas Machell noted that at Natland there was 'no vicar – prayers read by schoolmaster.' Some years earlier, from 1674 to 1683, Natland had in fact been home to Richard Frankland's Dissenting (Nonconformist) Northern Academy, the earliest of the remarkable Dissenting Academies: for almost a decade it was the privilege of Natland to give it shelter. Harris Manchester College, Oxford, founded as Manchester College in 1893, and since 1993 a full college of Oxford University, can trace its origins directly to the Dissenting Manchester Academy, founded in 1786, and beyond that, less directly, to Frankland's Academy: appropriately, a portrait of Frankland is displayed in the College Hall.

Richard Frankland had been educated at Christ's College, Cambridge, and had preached for short periods in Northumberland and Durham. In 1662 he was ejected from his living on grounds of Nonconformity, and returned to his native Rathmell, near Settle. It was at Rathmell, in 1670, that he founded his Academy. The first pupils were intended to enter the medical and legal professions, but soon young men who were training for the Presbyterian and Independent ministry began to be sent there. At first single-handed, and later with the help of tutors whom he had trained, Frankland lectured on logic, metaphysics, somatology (concerned with bodily and material existence), pneumatology (doctrine of the nature and operations of the spirit), natural philosophy, divinity, and chronology. Lectures were in Latin. Many pupils went on to the Scottish universities, where they received their degree after one session's attendance. According to Herbert McLachlan, in his *English Education Under the Test Acts* (Manchester: Manchester University Press, 1931), 'the scholarship of the tutors in the academies was at least equal to [that] of contemporary teachers in the universities, and their devotion to their work more conspicuous' (p. 18).

The Academy was carried on under considerable difficulties. Frankland apparently received a 'call' from a Dissenting congregation in Natland, and as a result the Northern Academy moved here early in 1674. Where the Academy was housed is not known. Canon Miller surmised that it might have been in Natland Hall; we know, however, that in 1673 the Recorder of Kendal, Alan Prickett, was living there. No doubt the pupils were boarded out, as they were at Hawkshead Grammar School when William Wordsworth attended in 1780s. The Kendal Justices were soon aware of the

Natland School 1909. Top row: Dick Graham, S. Abatson, Birt Winder, P. Gray, C. Clark, C. Mason, D. Trotter, Alfred Robinson. 2nd row: Ronnie Mattocks, John Hayhurst, Geo. Dixon, Dick Armer, John Little, Tom Mason. 3rd row: Mary Thewlis, Lillian Robinson, Nellie Parker, Phoebe Armer, Susie Graham, Madge Swinglehurst, Mary Ewan, Mabel Parker, Alan Ewan. 4th row: ?, Vincent Pinch, Edward Kendal, Edward Miller, Bert Stevenson, Stan Ducksbury, H. Downham, Miss F. Birchall. Courtesy Christine Moore

Natland Schoolteachers 1916: Back row l to r: Miss Proctor, Mr. Woodburn, Miss Smith (Chief Constable's daughter), Mrs Pooley and Mr. Goodwin.
Courtesy late Mrs. Maples

presence of the law-breaker, but allowed Frankland to stay quietly till the next Quarter Sessions, at Michaelmas, when he must, in accordance with the so-called Five Mile Act of 1665, move at least five miles from the town. During the early days at Natland there were probably fewer than a dozen pupils. One parent, Oliver Heywood, had two sons at Natland, for whom he made a payment of £6 as 'quarterage.' In 1676 no fewer than six proceeded to Scotland to take degrees. On one occasion a boy drowned, and another narrowly escaped drowning, in the river Kent. Frankland had several children of his own – five, according to the *Dictionary of National Biography*; when his eldest son John died, one of the students, Nathaniel Heywood, wrote, 'He was the strongest man of his age in or about Natland, and excelled all of us in exercise of body – his distemper came by a strain got with leaping.'

The local Dissenting congregation apparently increased under Frankland's influence, and he preached not only in Natland but also in Kendal, Stainton and elsewhere. In 1683, however, he was forced to leave. The Northern Academy was transferred first to Calton Hall, in the parish of Kirkby Malham, and later that year to Dawson Fold in Crosthwaite. In September 1684 Frankland moved to Hartbarrow near Cartmel Fell; then yet again in November 1686 to Attercliffe near Sheffield. From October 24th 1682, when the last scholar was admitted at Natland, to November 8th 1686, only thirteen scholars were admitted; the move to Attercliffe, however, was followed by a period of prosperity. The Academy finally returned to Rathmell. Frankland died, apparently surrounded by his scholars, on October 1st 1698, and was buried in Giggleswick Church.

Under Frankland's old pupil John Chorlton, who had entered at Natland in 1682, the Northern Academy was transferred to Manchester. Among the students at this early Manchester Academy was Thomas Dixon, who in turn started an Academy at Whitehaven, Cumberland. One of Dixon's pupils was Caleb Rotherham, who in 1716 became a Dissenting minister in Kendal, and was responsible for the building, in 1720, of the present Unitarian Church off the Market Place. Thirteen years later Rotherham himself set up an Academy that carried on until a few months after his death in 1752.

NATLAND VILLAGE SCHOOL

Schooling in Natland has had a chequered history. As we have seen, Machell mentions the presence of a 'schoolmaster' in 1691. I have been told that, at some time in the past, there was a 'Dame school' in the cottage attached to Natland Abbey, in which, presumably, an elderly woman gave a few children the rudiments of education. At some date it was reported that there was a

Day School with an average attendance of 27, and a Sunday School at which the average number of pupils was 20. It appears that there was a 'Parochial Library' of about twenty volumes, with a few pamphlets, under the care of the Master, and occasionally used. In 1818 the Brougham Committee on Education, chaired by Henry Brougham, M.P. for Westmorland, called for Parochial Returns: the National Society archives show that there was 'A Day School at Natland at which 35 children are taught by a Master, who had £39 per annum out of an estate, and a Sunday School, consisting of 34 boys and girls, the Master of whom received £3 from the same estate and was assisted by two ladies.' There is no mention of where, or under what conditions, the Master taught his pupils. A purpose-built School was opened in 1825, next door to the new Church. We do not know how much it cost or what accommodation it provided, or even for certain who was the first Headmaster; but we do know that by 1829 the Head was Robert Townson. The earliest School logbook that survives, recording daily activities and events, begins in 1878.

The Education Enquiry of 1833 showed that in Natland there was 'one day and Sunday School attended by 25 males and 13 females daily and by 18 males and 10 females on Sunday which was partly supported by an endowment arising from an estate in the chapelry, for which children of the poor were instructed gratuitously; others paid a small quarterage; a small library of 106 volumes was attached for the use of the school and the village generally.' In 1846-47 the schoolmaster was paid £55 per annum out of the endowment and payments from children. At this time, of course, education was neither free nor compulsory, and the early logbooks show that at Natland many of the older children only attended part time, either because their parents could not afford the 'school pence,' or because they were employed part-time either in farm work or milk delivery, or at the Sedgwick Gunpowder Works. The School was often closed early to allow the building to be used for other purposes, and there were half- or whole holidays for a variety of reasons.

The Elementary Education Act of 1870 created School Boards throughout the country, making education compulsory for children of 5 to 13 years, with a place in an elementary school for every child of school age. An Act of 1891 abolished school fees and an Act of 1902 authorised the levying of an Education Rate. The first Inspectors from the Board of Education visited Natland School in 1878. The School began to be paid according to results, becoming less dependent on the Church. In the early days the School depended heavily on monitors and pupil-teachers, but the rising number of pupils persuaded the School Managers to increase full-time staff.

The children of the gypsies who wintered in Natland were desperately in need of education, leading one contemporary to remark contemptuously,

'No kindness can scarcely thaw the frosts of their innate superstition and prejudice, nor any wholesome nutrient entice their low grovelling minds from feeding upon the husks of ignorance.' No doubt the gypsy children were left largely to their own devices. School numbers increased with the development of Helmside and Oxenholme. The School was partially rebuilt and enlarged, at a cost of £230, towards which the railway company made a grant. Now there was accommodation for 90 scholars, under an efficient master, Mr Edgar Mellor. In 1879 the Church authorities built a house for the use of the schoolmaster, the principal subscriber being Mrs Metcalfe of Prizet; as we have seen, in 1882 it was converted temporarily into a home for the reception of orphaned and destitute boys until St Mark's Home was built. The arrival of the 'Home boys' added to the accommodation problem, and for a time the Vicar allowed his Vicarage washhouse to be used as a classroom. By 1907 fifteen of the bigger 'Home boys' were transferred to Crosscrake School. By 1909 new classroom accommodation was built here; and in 1914 Natland School, 'mixed and infants,' could accommodate 184 pupils, with an average attendance of 115. The Headmaster at this time was John Goodwin, the infants being taught by Miss Elizabeth Procter. In 1917 the School acquired a garden, and gardening became a useful and important part of the curriculum.

Mr Goodwin left in the May of 1919, having served as Headmaster since 1893, and was succeeded by Mr F.H. Corrie. That year there were usually about 93 on the roll, and in June the average attendance was 89% over three years of age: obviously there were some very young pupils. On June 10th 1919, at 11.45 am, the children were arranged near the school flag. Patriotic sons were sung, and the Vicar, the Rev. Miller, addressed the children on the significance of the Peace Treaty; a half-holiday followed. Later, from August 19th to 22nd, the children had an extended holiday for the Peace Celebrations. The first anniversary of Armistice Day was observed with a service of silence and remembrance, when hymns were sung, the Roll of Honour read out, and a suitable address given to the children. The School Garden was extended and planted with fruit trees. In the following year, 1920, the logbook contains the first mention of a County Minor Scholarship, won by Catherine Corrie, the Head's daughter, who went on to Kendal Girls' High School. There is also the first mention of a School Caretaker – though there must have been one previously – and the regulations concerning the cleaning of schools are explained in detail. Each week several senior girls attended the Milnthorpe Centre for a cookery course, travelling from Oxenholme by the 8.38 am Furness train, and returning to Oxenholme at 3.30 pm. The eldest girl was responsible for the Cookery Register, and as far as she was able took charge of the other girls.

That May, Empire Day was observed with the National Anthem, patriotic songs, and an address by the Rev. Miller. Suitable lessons were given through the day emphasising the responsibilities of Empire. Mr Corrie, with an unnamed assistant, took the Seniors and Juniors, whilst the Infants continued to be ably taught by Miss Procter. Miss Proctor had taught at the School since October 10th 1907, the year in which the Rev. Miller had arrived in Natland, her only qualification being that she had been vaccinated. Her methods would seem strange today, but they certainly worked: without exception her pupils learned to read and write. Moreover, she was able to keep abreast of the times, as she could keep an eye on village affairs from the window facing the village Green. In 1935 the school was wired for electric lighting, a great improvement on the former acetylene gas, and a new heating boiler was installed. In 1938 the playground was extended.

Whereas the First World War passed almost without remark in the logbook, the Second War made a much greater impact, as it did in village life in general. The Second World War came to the people as never before in history. In August 1939 the School had an air-raid warning rehearsal, and was closed from September 1st to the 6th for the national emergency, when evacuees poured into all our country districts. By September 7th School numbers had risen to 150, literally overnight, though by the following January a reshuffle had reduced the numbers to 128. That year the logbook contains the first reference to diphtheria immunisation. In December Mr Corrie left Natland, and in April 1941 Mr E.T. Ward took over the Headship.

In February 1941 a 'wireless' set was installed, Canon Miller having raised the necessary quota towards this. The first broadcast heard was at 10.30 am – the 'Service for Schools' – after which Canon Miller spoke of 'the power and influence of the unseen.' Which probably puzzled a few of the children. More evacuees arrived from Barrow-in-Furness that spring, the number on roll reaching 163; a room at Abbey Cottage was used for a while as an overflow classroom till the Barrow children, many of whom were Roman Catholics, were moved to Sedgwick. Rabbit keeping was started, but with what success we are not told. A frequent entry in the logbook related to the absence of a particular member of staff when her husband was on leave. Extra staff had of course come with the evacuees. On D-Day, June 6th 1944, senior pupils followed the fortunes of the invasion on the 'wireless.'

In 1945 my husband Sam Inglesfield took over as Headmaster. We soon hear of changes. Sam believed in the involvement of parents, believing that they should feel part of the School's life, taking an active interest in their children's education. A Parent-Teachers Association was started, and was welcomed with great enthusiasm. This was a gallant body, which was to work with great willingness for the good of the School, right up to the present day: how they have worked! Staff meetings were held to discuss

School affairs. By December 1945 further changes had taken place – a Christmas Party, a School Carol Service and a Prizegiving. An era ended with the retirement of Miss Procter after thirty-nine years in the Infants department. Not that she was any less busy in retirement – the village obtained a full-time dispenser of news. She had her regular route round the village. When we left the School House and moved to our house down Hawes Lane, we found we missed out on Miss Proctor's visits. After we told her this, we were occasionally included on her circuit for really world-shattering items of news. Miss Procter died in 1962, but she will be long remembered, for she was a real character.

For some time after the War food was severely rationed. The School logbook records that a parcel arrived from Canada for distribution amongst the scholars: this contained milk powder, and the children got $1\frac{3}{4}$ pounds each. Standard tests were being used for the first time for the assessment of the children's progress. The 1944 Education Act had a profound effect on schools throughout the country. Every Education Authority had to ensure that for every child over the age of 11 there was a place in a secondary school. Westmorland Education Authority was always on the ball: it was a wonderful authority. They had already drawn up and implemented a scheme for the selection, at 11-plus, of children thought suitable for Grammar School education, and had also set up two 'Modern Schools' in Kendal, one for girls in the former premises of the Wesleyan Methodist Day School just off Kendal Green, and one for boys in the premises of the old Quaker Grammar School just off Stramongate. By 1957 all the older children were being schooled in Kendal, which made a terrific change in a country School like Natland. The number on roll, which stood at just over 60 in the early 1950s, fell to only 44; but within ten years this number almost doubled, as both Natland and Oxenholme grew apace.

Also on the books – every Local Education Authority had to draw up, publish and submit a Development Plan, outlining its intentions for every school in its area. Natland was to become a Church of England Voluntary Aided Mixed Primary School of two classes, for about 60 children. It was pointed out that the site on which the old School was built, 0.42 acres in area, was too small and wouldn't allow for expansion, and the Plan proposed that the School should be rebuilt on a new and larger site. The estimated cost at that time, 1946, was £1,500 for the site, and £9,700 for the buildings: more of that later.

In 1947 there was the first School Sports Day, held on Mr Bindloss's field, where the new School now stands. With the help of the PTA this proved a most popular event, with races, prizes, tea and ices free for all the children (and at a small charge for everyone else), a Punch and Judy show, a fancy dress parade, and a wild flower competition: with good weather, it was a

Natland School 1956. Top row: Barry Almeida, Robert Ephgrave, Bernard Crowhurst, David Dowker, Eldred Himsworth, Malcolm Brown, Alan Huck, David Benson, Robert Inglesfield, James Duff, Stephen Bleasdale. 2nd row: Murdoch Brown, Alfred Row, Terry Swainbank, Ian Dowker, Duncan Preston, Mabel Kirk, Robert Charnley, Valerie Gowdie. 3rd row: Pauline Pears, Carol Edwards, Kathleen Nicholson, Pat Cheeseman, Elizabeth Armer, Mr. Heighton, Anne Charnley, Susan Hodgson, Jennifer Addison, Christine Nicholson.

Courtesy late Mrs. Maples

Natland School Sports – early 1950s – held in the field where the school is now. L to r: Philip Ball, Pauline Simkiss, David Saul, Judith Kendal and ?.

Courtesy Philip Ball

super day for everybody. In later years Sports Day developed into a three-cornered sports contest with Crosscrake and Old Hutton Schools, being held at each in turn.

The School canteen was started in 1949, using a converted classroom for the kitchen. Mrs Simkiss was the first cook, and dinners were also made for Crosscrake and Old Hutton Schools, usually being transported by whoever ran the village shop. School dinner cost 5d per day, though this was heavily subsidised: the meal was attractive, varied and balanced. (Today school dinner costs £1.60p, so the week's dinner money will be £8 – quite a lot if one has a few children. The School canteen is now run by Joan Withers, and also supplies meals for St. Thomas's School in Kendal. The meals remain very good, with varied and healthy menus, so I hear.) This was an excellent service for those unable to reach home during the dinner hour: these children had previously brought sandwiches. In fact most children stayed for school dinners, including the Headmaster's children, who lived only just across the Green. The boys from St. Mark's Home, on the other hand, went back for their dinner.

Ever more activities were introduced – a percussion band, puppetry; School concerts became a greater delight year by year, and each Open Day more open to admiration. Prizes and cups were regularly won by the School at the Westmorland Horticultural Show. Rosehips were collected, at 3d per pound, later 4d, with badges awarded for a total of 12 pounds. Rosehip collecting played havoc with children's clothes!

For some time plans had been discussed for the installation of water closets in the School. Funds were raised by various 'efforts' and subscriptions. The six closets, with accompanying water supply and drainage, were installed entirely by voluntary work, with an eager band of parents meeting every evening, weather permitting. Work was completed on June 16th 1952. A further landmark in 1952 was the introduction of the visiting Library Van. Swimming had long been a popular weekly event, with a trip to the Kendal Baths, and that July Natland won four out of five firsts at the Inter-Schools Swimming Gala. Soon after the Coronation of Queen Elizabeth II in June 1953, a party of children was taken to see the colour film 'A Queen is Crowned;' to mark the occasion the PTA presented the School with two electric clocks. Another film spotlighted 'The Conquest of Everest.'

That year also marked the occasion of the first visit of Father Christmas to the Christmas Party. Behind the scenes there was the furtive putting-on of his regalia – and then into action, Father Christmas greeting a crowd of excited children. On one occasion there were an awkward moment as a small boy recognised his Dad – either by his trouser turn-ups or his shoes – we didn't ascertain which. After that we were lucky to have John Pickthall, who farmed down at Hincaster, as Father Christmas: with his round smiling face, and always a friendly word to each child, John was a great success. The children, the caretaker and friend of all Mrs James, the canteen staff, and the teachers – Father Christmas remembered them all. In 1954 the School Garden, which had been rented from Natland Park farm, was sold. Eventually Miss Mallabar, Children's Officer for the Church of England's Children's Society, built a bungalow there, with the benefit of the old School Garden fruit trees.

Sam Inglesfield left in December 1956: I seem to have given more details of his Headship, as he instituted so many changes, many of which have endured over the years. Sam became Head of the Parish Church School in Kendal, and later he moved with the School to brand-new open-plan premises at Heron Hill – the old buildings becoming Kirkland Hall, an annexe to the Parish Hall. After Sam left Natland a supply teacher, Miss Owen, took temporary charge at Natland until Mr Haydon Moore arrived in April. Sadly he was only here a short time – he died suddenly in January 1959. Mr Colin Heighton, a very gifted assistant at Natland School for many years, stayed on as Acting Head till the end of the school year.

There were 44 on the roll when Mr J.R.B. Storm came as Headmaster in September 1959, and during the next few years there were several innovations. For some years the Library Van had been available to the children, but now the service was extended to the villagers, with fortnightly visits. A mobile Dental Surgery arrived in 1960, but the service was short-lived; instead children attended the School Dental Clinic off Stramongate in Kendal. The School acquired a new record player. Numbers dropped dramatically to 29 when St. Mark's Home was closed temporarily in October 1960. A year or two later a special bus was detailed to take the children to the Baths: they had previously had some cold wet walks to and from the bus at Helmside. Mr Storm met troubles during the spring of 1963: there were prolonged frosts that year, and the lavatories froze; and on one memorable day the cold water supply failed in the morning, and the electricity went off in the afternoon. What a day! A fire in the boiler house destroyed half a ladder and all the firewood, following a WI concert the previous evening. The Headmaster rather blamed the WI, though he didn't accuse us openly. This was certainly an opportune moment for the first reference in the logbook to a new School, though this had been mooted for at least ten years previously.

Mr Laurie Hicks took over the Headship in 1964, and right from the start he was able to look forward to moving into new premises. The site, consisting of 1.75 acres, was just round the corner from the old School – in fact, on the old School sports field. The Foundation Stone was laid by Colonel Crewdson on July 6th 1964. There was a service in the Church, then a procession of children, staff, parents and friends, to the site. The children laid individual stones. The brochure told us:

> The new Church of England School at Natland is situated in the centre of the village, well sited for all the children likely to attend and conveniently close to the Church. The School building will cover an area of almost 5,000 sq. ft, and will accommodate 80 pupils in three classrooms – the Infants classroom and ancillary accommodation being a separate unit and linked by a covered way to the school buildings. A well-equipped kitchen will serve meals directly to a central space which forms a link between the Junior classrooms, and this is divided from them by sliding/folding screens. The site has an area of 13/8 acres. A tar paved area will be provided, with a partly enclosed paved court with flowering shrubs and bench seating as a feature. The School will be heated by means of an oil-fired system. The architects were Charles L. Mawson, ARIBA, and Charles G. Dean, Dip. Arch., ARIBA, of Hargreaves and Mawson, Kendal, and the general contractor was W.H. Ainsworth & Co. Ltd, Kendal.

The following spring the children planted trees, roses and shrubs in their new grounds. On June 10th 1967 St. Mark's Church of England Primary School, Natland, was dedicated and opened by the Bishop of Carlisle. There was a service in the Church, further ceremony in the new School, and tea to follow in the old School. Two days later, on the Monday, the children and staff moved all the School fittings and materials for their first day in the new building. The new School cost in the region of £31,000, the Church paying

Front of new School.

Old School demolished.

Westmorland Gazette.   *Courtesy Local Studies Section, Kendal Library*

Sam opening the School library in 1981. Looking on is Laurie Hicks standing immediately behind Sam, Mrs. Hicks, myself, Rev. Stannard and children.

Courtesy Philip Ball

about a quarter of this under the Barchester Scheme. Once the new School was open and in use, the old building was sold for £1,800, and in May 1969 it was demolished – a sad sight for many of us. Three houses were subsequently built on the site. In 1981 the *Westmorland Gazette* reported the opening of a new School library. Sam Inglesfield, who performed the opening ceremony, remarked in his speech that he deplored the cuts in education expenditure, while Mr Hicks praised the PTA for seeing the project through.

New housing brought an increase in School numbers: in September 1967 there were 64 on the roll, and two years later there were 89. Even the new School proved inadequate, and plans were made for an extension to provide two more classrooms. W.R. Wark was architect, and Greenholme Construction was General Contractor. On St. Mark's Day, April 25th 1972, the new premises were dedicated and opened by the Bishop of Penrith, the Right Reverend Edward Pugh. For a time a temporary mobile classroom was erected on the edge of the playing field, though this was removed in the autumn of 1985. By the following year there were plans for a small extension to the block of two classrooms opened in 1972, providing improved access as well as a useful 'wet area' for teaching art and craft. There was no hope of a grant, but the Diocese offered a low-interest loan to cover half the cost, if the School and/or the Church could raise the rest. A Fund Raising Committee consisting of some of the Governors, staff and parents, went ahead with various 'efforts,' and over £4,000 was raised in two years. Work was completed in 1989, and in the following year the balance was raised and the loan paid off. Natland School is now in the hands of twelve local Governors, half of them appointed by the Church, with the Vicar as an *ex officio* member. Mike Nelson was a long-serving Chairman. Mr Chandler took over as Headmaster in 1984 and retired in 2005 and was followed by Peter Barfoot. Mrs Cheeseman, for many years a very popular caretaker, retired. Meanwhile the PTA raised funds to purchase books, computers, printers and a sound system, bringing Natland School 'bang up-to-date.'

The School logbooks record frequent interruptions of daily routine, for one reason or another. Merit holidays, royal weddings and funerals, coronations, rummage sales, parochial teas, choir trips, Kendal Show Day, Ascension Day, Armistice Day: all special days had to be observed – really, never a dull moment. There were visitors to the School, increasingly frequent in latter years as education officials proliferated, always creating distraction. There were frequent visits by the Vicar and the School Managers, who often dropped in to inspect the registers, His or Her Majesty's Inspectors, the School Attendance Officer, Diocesan Religious Inspector, Medical Officer, Dental Inspector, Physical Training Organiser, District Nurse (for weighing, head-inspections etc.), Speech Therapist, Music Organiser, Youth

School House in 2006 with Village Hall to the left.
Seat in foreground is memorial to Pearson Charnley.

Employment Officer, Psychologist, School Meals Organiser – not forgetting the piano-tuner, whose visits are recorded with rather surprising frequency.

There have been 'royal' occasions, too. In June 1974, the Queen was travelling north to carry out various engagements, and was coming to Oxenholme Station. It was decided where the children would get the best view, and a letter was sent to Buckingham Palace, with a request for a special wave if possible. So, on that wonderfully exciting morning the children made their way to the station, armed with enormous flags and banners. They hoped the Queen would remember their request. The Queen managed to squeeze a few minutes out of a very tight schedule to speak to some of the children, and particularly the Brownies. And later she sent them a letter saying how much she had enjoyed seeing them, and thanking them for their warm welcome. Years later, on November 21st 2003, the Queen's cousin the Duke of Kent came to Kendal to visit Cancer Care, the winner of the highly prized Queen's Golden Jubilee Award for Voluntary Service. The Duke's next stop was Natland School: here he graciously opened the new School Hall. The building, which cost £200,000, partly raised through a fund-raising campaign, had been completed the previous summer. Having toured the School and chatted to the pupils, the Duke stayed on for lunch – not, admittedly, the same fare as the children, but a special buffet prepared by the School cook. He went on to visit Bendrigg Lodge, Old Hutton, where the Bendrigg Trust specialises in running courses and activities for disabled and disadvantaged young people.

The logbooks record numerous outings and School trips – ranging from nature walks to observe the changing seasons, and visits to Newlands Poultry Farm and Kendal Museum, to full-day excursions to the seaside at Morecambe or Heysham Head, and to Grizedale Forest, the Roman Wall, York and Edinburgh.

The last fifty years have been noticeably free from the outbreaks of scarlet fever, diphtheria and measles that are mentioned in the earlier books; even typhoid fever and smallpox occasionally raised their ugly heads. Sores and ringworm had been commonplace. During the last War there were outbreaks of scabies – blamed on the evacuees – maybe too common to record in earlier days. Early entries refer to pupils staying off School because of bad weather – probably due to lack of suitable clothing. Thick coats would be a luxury for the few, and right into the 1920s clogs were normal footwear for country children.

LIFE IN THE SCHOOL HOUSE

Though my husband Sam took over as Headmaster of Natland School in 1945, we had to wait till the spring of 1948 before we moved in: meanwhile we lived in Enyeat Cottage in Endmoor. Before we moved into the School House a little modernising took place: a huge old kitchen range was removed and a more modern one – still an awkward affair – installed. I had never had to 'pull dampers' to heat an oven. On one unfortunate occasion, whilst doing this, I pulled back and then ricocheted, breaking my nose on the metal mantelpiece. There was a hot water system and a cylinder cupboard of sorts. Whist Drives were held to raise money for the School House Bathroom Fund.

The bathroom was duly completed in spring 1949, built by a firm from Milnthorpe, I think – a more local firm would perhaps have been wiser. What a mess we had to contend with, especially difficult with a toddler and a baby in the house. The builders broke through the main wall, on the east side, coinciding with a strong east wind. They failed to tie the building properly into the main wall of the house, and before long the whole structure broke away, leaving a gap, while a crack developed in the cement floor. The water pipes were supported by six-inch nails, looped up! The builders had completely forgotten to install electricity. Then there was further trouble: the wall separating the bathroom and toilet, we discovered, was one length of a brick too short, and a certain tall man had to demonstrate to the Diocesan Architect how he couldn't shut the door whilst in a sitting position! There was no room for any heating apparatus, and when a hard frost burst the pipes, the water drained away in no time through the cracked floor. Of course the bathroom represented a great advance on the earlier bucket-toilet arrangements. In those days before central heating the School House was very cold.

When the Vicarage barn immediately behind the house was converted into the Village Hall, our garden, which had extended along the side of the barn and across the far end, was lost to the new car park. In its place we were given a patch of ground that had always been the Vicarage rubbish dump, which wasn't 'much cop.' We did our best with it. The clothes-posts had, of course, to be moved there, and a message was brought asking that the Inglesfield washing might be kept out of sight from the Vicarage. I thought 'Who the —— do they think they are?,' and sent a curt message back, that as I was expecting my third child, Christopher and there would soon be nappies on the washing line – my flags of rejoicing – which would be hung out to get the best drying conditions. We eventually moved out in January 1957. Various structural alterations were made before the Moore family moved in at Easter. Mr Storm's family lived there throughout his term of service. The Hicks family stayed there till the spring of 1967, when they bought a modern house up the village. The School House was eventually sold to the Diocese in 1968, and further alterations were carried out, the house becoming a residence for retired clergy. Later it was sold privately.

Chapter 9

ORGANISATIONS, INTERESTS AND ENTERTAINMENTS

THE VILLAGE HALL

The village School had always served as a public hall, which caused a great deal of disruption, with desks and other equipment having to be moved when rooms were needed for some function. For years there had been talk of a purpose-built Village Hall, but in the end the idea was shelved till costs were less prohibitive – and Natland had to make do with a converted barn. The Vicarage barn had been used by the Vicar as a garage, and it was decided that a new garage should be built closer to the Vicarage. After nine years of fund-raising by all ways and means, followed by the actual conversion, the Village Hall Committee had the satisfaction of having created a Village Hall that would serve for the time being. The Mayor of Kendal, Mrs M.L. Pennington, accompanied by the Mayoress, her daughter Mrs A. Thompson, opened the Hall, and were presented with bouquets by Ann Charnley.

The barn had been bought for £250, towards which the Ministry of Education contributed £83. The conversion cost £1,275, including a £419 conversion grant from the Ministry. There was space for 135 seats. The flooring was of Japanese oak strip. The kitchen and cloakroom were only temporary affairs. The architect was Mr G.C. Jackson of Kendal, and the builder Arthur Brown of Natland. The old School House garden was levelled for a car park. The Women's Institute had done a great deal in raising money for the Hall, and has been one of the principal bodies using it. Over the years various modifications have been made, including overhead electric heating. The inadequate kitchen was always a source of dissatisfaction. The enthusiastic young members of the Badminton Club were the prime movers in raising funds for a new kitchen and cloakroom extension, their chief effort being a sponsored walk in June 1968. The day proved to be the hottest of that summer, but a gallant turnout of villagers and friends completed their twenty miles, nearly to a man. Refreshments were supplied *en route* – squash, apples, sweets and hot soup, to keep spirits up. The elder members of the community prepared an enormous buffet meal for the walkers and helpers – and afterwards some of the young lads, including my youngest son Christopher, went off to help in the hayfields for the rest of the evening. This effort raised £400, and the day was especially memorable for its spirit of friendship and *esprit de corps*. Pearson Charnley carried out the building work, and Philip Ball did the 'electrics,' both working voluntarily, and the extension was already in use by the autumn.

In the mid-1960s the hall was extended by the addition of a temporary timber annexe, and in the 1980s new toilets were installed. But problems remained, and by the late 1990s there were plans for major alterations. The statement supporting the Planning Application made in September 1997 pointed out that the main hall was not large enough to accommodate a range of activities, such as table tennis, badminton, and line-dancing. Groups using the annexe had to enter the main hall to access the toilets and kitchen, resulting in a certain amount of disturbance. Furthermore, the Village Hall was not accessible by disabled people, and was not up to the current standards in energy efficiency. The Hall and annexe were being used during the week by the following organisations and groups: the Playgroup, the Monday Club, the Table Tennis Club, the Badmington Club, the Rainbows, the Women's Institute, University of the Third Age, Line and Country Dancing. At the weekends, moreover, the Hall was used for rummage sales, children's parties and private hire. Planning permission was granted, and alterations were carried out, at a final cost in the region of £90,000. It was money well spent. The modernised building is in constant use.

WOMEN'S INSTITUTE

In 1969 the Women's Institute, founded in 1919, celebrated its fiftieth anniversary. The various local WIs were asked to produce accounts of their activities and the changes in village life during this period, and these records were deposited at the Kendal Archives Office.

The first recorded meeting of Natland and Oxenholme WI was a general meeting held in the Railway Mission hall at Oxenholme on October 20th 1921, with Mrs Page of Brough Fold in the Chair. The speaker was Mrs Nugent Harris, Chief Organiser of the National Federation of Women's Institutes. It was decided to hold meetings on the third Friday of each month, the first being on November 4th 1921 (which wasn't the third Friday!), with Mrs Keesey as President. The annual subscription was 2s 6d, and there were 43 members. These meetings continued over the years, but lapsed during the Second World War from December 1942. In July 1946 Mrs Crewdson rallied a group of women – 25 to be exact – and the WI got off to a fresh start, with Mrs Ewan as President. Numbers fluctuated over the years. By 1969 we had 58 members, with an average attendance of 40. Many Kendal women wished to join us, and they were very welcome; but it was decided to restrict the town membership to 20 in order to maintain the WI's country character. The subscription had risen to 10s by this stage, and many of us felt that this was insufficient. Until the conversion of the Village Hall meetings were held in the old School. Meetings now took place on the third Wednesday of each month, except for December, when the meeting

WI Members at Westmorland County Show, Shap Road, Kendal in the 1960s.
In the picture are Mrs. Ball, Mrs. Mary Frearson, Mrs. Olive Clarke
and Mrs. Kathleen Brown.

Westmorland Gazette.   *Courtesy Philip Ball*

was brought forward by a week to avoid the Christmas rush. On the afternoon before the meeting two or three members prepared the room, and in the course of the meeting tea and biscuits were served for 6d per head. A Committee of twelve was elected by ballot at the AGM in November, after which the various officers were elected. Committee meetings were held each month.

Natland WI had its own choir, led by Daphne Lester, who was Music mistress at Kendal High School, which was regularly successful at the Mary Wakefield Festival. Several members took part in the Country Produce and Handicraft competitions at the Westmorland County Show. The programmes for the monthly meetings covered a wide variety of talks – far from the jam-making image of earlier years. The Natland and Oxenholme Women's Institute continues to flourish: at present Kirsten Cannon is President, and Margaret Lancaster, Secretary.

Going back to earlier years – I must mention two members who made a name for themselves in the dramatic line: both should have gone on the stage. At a WI concert in Kendal two of our members, Elsie Tatham and Ena Brown, gave a memorable rendering of the old song, 'There's a hole in my bucket, dear Lisa, dear Lisa.' Performing with perfect timing, they were unbelievably funny, and many members of the audience laughed till they cried. At a WI concert in Natland several members did a spirited rendering of the can-can, at the end of which Ena, already forty-four years old, did the 'splits.' Now 91, she is still going strong.

British Legion, W.R.V.S. and Meals on Wheels

The Natland men's branch of the British Legion amalgamated with the Kendal branch in the 1960s, but the Natland and Sedgwick women's branch carried on successfully, with 25 or 30 members at one time. Funds raised for the Women's Section Scheme were used for the provision of rest homes, flats, supplementary allowances for widows and so on. The WRVS is no longer active in Natland, apart from the Meals on Wheels service. Meals are transported from the Kendal Day Centre to the village shop, from where they are collected by volunteers. There are usually about a dozen recipients, in an area that includes Sedgwick, Hincaster and Endmoor. At present meals cost £1.50p.

Mr. Broadbent from the PO loading meals to deliver to Crosscrake.
Courtesy late Mrs. Maples

Natland Monday Club

After he retired in 1980 Sam Inglesfield started the Natland Monday Club, for retired people. Monday afternoon was chosen as a convenient time for the monthly meetings – hence the name. The Club has continued to thrive over the years. At present Mrs Margaret Cummings is Chair, and Mrs Midge Fairhurst, Secretary. There are talks on varied subjects, slideshows, the occasional outing, quizzes and whatever.

SCOUTING AND GUIDING

Natland has had Boy Scouts, Girl Guides and Brownies at one time or another, but curiously enough never Wolf Cubs. Whilst Mr Ward was the Headmaster of the Natland School he ran a Boy Scout Troop for a time. Much detective work uncovered the fact that Mrs Graham of Brigsteer, who was the elder Miss Anson of Windy Brow before her marriage, started the first Girl Guide Company here in 1921. Her first Lieutenant was Miss Kendal of Natland Park, and her Patrol Leaders were Gladys Armer, later Mrs Dixon of Sedgwick, and Alice Hodgson, later Mrs George. Laura Pinch, later Mrs Crabtree, was one of the first members, and it was she who took the part of 'Bonnie Jane of Natland' at the Village Fair organised by the WI in 1935. When Mrs Anson became District Commissioner she handed the Captaincy to her younger sister, who on her marriage in the late 1920s closed the Company. Miss Evelyn Crewdson of Helme Lodge captained a

Guides and Brownies in mid-1980s pictured after presenting the name plaque to the Village Hall.
Back row: Guides - Mrs. Rosemary Usher, Rebecca Rigg, Victoria Muir, Sarah Langstaff,
Andrea Webster, Pearson Charnley, Jane Usher (Ranger), Julie Baxter, Maddy Evans,
Dawn Nicholson (Ranger) and Marie Nicholson (Unit Helper – Brownies)
Middle row: Ailie Shackleton, ?, Jeanette Bannister, Helen Wells, Kate Holmes, Tracy Archibald,
Lindsay Gaskell and Ann Tilney (Brown Owl)
Brownies - Elinor Jayne (2nd row 2nd left), Joanna Evans, Catherine Carter, ? ?
Front row: Ruth Shippon, Pippa Jayne, Amanda Brying, Stephanie Bannister and Helen Carter.
Westmorland Gazette   *Courtesy Local Studies Section, Kendal Library*

new Company from 1930 till her marriage in about 1937, and Miss Dinsdale of Kendal carried on till just after the War. Miss Crewdson had a jaunty open car, very racy for those days. She would pack in a large number of hefty GGs to deliver them home after the meeting. This ride home had always proved very hilarious, and was remembered long after by those involved. In 1956 Miss Kathleen Ingram and Miss Wendy Balmer were able to form another Company, which lasted many years. This was eventually taken over by Mrs Rosemary Usher.

CRAFT CLASSES

I have failed to trace any record of adult classes that were run in Natland in earlier days: it is surprisingly difficult to turn up such information. For some years there was an embroidery class run by the Crosscrake WI, in the Reading Room at Oxenholme, with Mrs Whiteman as teacher. She had taught the Misses Elsie and Edith Whittle of Beetham, who in turn, for twelve wonderful winters, took our Craft Class, first in the old School and then in the Village Hall. They worked so hard themselves, producing an enormous range of beautiful examples to help us and give us ideas. No matter what obscure craft one might wish to do – you name it – they taught it. At present Rosemary Usher runs a Craft Club in the Village Hall every Wednesday afternoon, members taking along whatever needlework they happen to be doing.

KEEP FIT

In the 1960s there was also a swinging Keep Fit class in the Village Hall, run by Mrs Eunice Rodgers of Prizet. Members gave demonstrations for charity. Later, in the 80s, Alison Richardson took Keep Fit classes, which were so energetic that some of the older keep-fitters had a struggle walking back up the hill.

NATLAND SPORTS AND FLOWER SHOW

Information about the early Natland Sports is almost non-existent. About the turn of the twentieth century Natland Sports owned a marquee that was stored in the Vicarage barn. At different times the Sports were held in the Natland Hall field called Jermett, and in Jack Huck's field at Barrows Green. When digging in our garden down Hawes Lane, years ago, I unearthed a 'Gents' notice that must have been a relic of the Sports, though there is no record of them having been held there. Soon after the last War, Natland Sports were restarted by a few enthusiasts. Held in one of Mr Kendal's fields at Natland Park, the Sports quickly grew more ambitious, including a

Flower Show in early 1990s.
Ingrid Beattie (Assistant Secretary), Hubert Williams (Vegetable Judge),
Pearson Charnley (Show Chairman) and Archie Beattie (Show Secretary),
Westmorland Gazette   *Courtesy Local Studies Section, Kendal Library*

hound-trail, track events, a guide race onto Helm, a pony gymkhana, a baby show, and on one occasion even motor-cycle racing. There was a beer tent too. The Sports were financed largely by whist drives and similar events. But public support flagged, and about the mid-1950s the Sports Funds were passed to the Flower Show Committee, which proceeded to form the Natland Horticultural Society. For some years a successful Flower Show was held, which, like the Sports, was supported keenly for a time, before interest fell off. The last Flower Show took place in the 1990s. The Society was wound up, and the various trophies were returned to their donors. It seems a pity that these things disappear: perhaps increased car ownership is partly to blame, encouraging people to go further afield for their entertainment.

Bonfire Night

For centuries a bonfire must have been lit here on November 5th. In the past this always took place on the Green, leaving a scarred area that never recovered till the next conflagration. About 1960 the bonfire site was sensibly moved to St. Mark's Home field. At one time village boys building the bonfire used to cut gorse bushes on Helm, dragging them down the lane on ropes trailing behind their bikes. I can remember staying at Natland over the time of Bonfire Night when I was very young. Fireworks were then few and less sophisticated. One of the main sources of excitement came from the lighting of rolled newspapers, which were flourished as burning brands, the bearers racing round with much yelling. This terrified me, as I'd never seen anything worse than a sparkler.

ENTERTAINMENTS

Mr Sill told me that children used to play games such as 'Guinea Pig,' or its alternative name, 'Spell and Knur' – or was it 'Knell and Spur'? This game, which seems to have been similar to rounders, was always played on the corner of the Green by the Church. There was also 'Ducky Stone,' traditionally played near where Mrs George's bungalow stands. Mr Sill thought these games had gone out of fashion soon after the First World War. In the early years of the twentieth century children would trundle a hoop, known locally as a 'booley,' on the way to school: I can still recall the jangling sound that the booley made. In the 1950s one would often see, in the evenings, small gatherings of men in the field where the School now stands, playing quoits, or engaged in clay pigeon shooting.

At one time, apart from visits to relatives, few Natland families would go away on holiday. A day trip by train, or a Choir outing by 'chara' to Morecambe or Blackpool Illuminations, was excitement enough. On any warm summer's day we would see family groups going down to the river, with a basket of food for a picnic. The stretch above Robin Hood's Island was a favourite place for swimming and paddling. When the river was low it was possible for children to paddle, at some risk, across to the island itself. A typhoid scare at the time when Waterside in Kendal was being demolished put an end to bathing. Children could play safely all day up on Helm, taking food for picnics – and returning tired, in need of a bath, but happy. This probably wouldn't be wise today.

Mr Dick Holmes, who started the garden nursery, was apparently one of the first in Natland to own a 'wireless' set. Television has, of course, made a huge difference. It has certainly played some part in the loss of local dialect. I think the Croft family had the first TV set in Natland. As I have already mentioned, the village hired a set for the Coronation in 1953. Unfortunately my children had measles at the time, so we hired a small set of our own, inviting a few old neighbours round to watch. The previous year we had watched the funeral of King George VI on Jim Howson's set at Newlands bungalow. We bought a small set in the autumn of 1954, and later we acquired a more recent model from a friend. Village concerts, for fund-raising or fun, and dances of various kinds were much more frequent before the advent of television. In the early days of the PTA some of the members who had been to Butlin's Holiday Camp brought back the craze for American square-dancing, and for a time we had regular sessions. We also had traditional folk dancing, with the help of Mr and Mrs Robinson who lived on Natland Road, Kendal, and were real enthusiasts.

For a short time in the early 1950s, evenings were cheered once a week by the arrival of a fish-and-chip van. It didn't come at mealtime, but nevertheless we all dashed out for this weekly treat. Part of the fun was gathering on the Green and waiting our turn. Unfortunately the frying apparatus caught fire one evening, and the van went up in flames before our very eyes. Later a larger converted fish-and- chip bus used to come round.

STAGHOUNDS AND COCK-FIGHTING

Hunting was never a very conspicuous activity in Natland. The Lunesdale and Oxenholme Staghounds, with their kennels at Gatebeck near Endmoor, covered quite a wide area of country. The only local people connected with this hunt, as far as I can gather, were the Temples of Oxenholme and the Heatons of Prizet. Though Prizet was outside the parish, the Heatons were always closely associated with Natland affairs. The Oxenholme Hunt carried on till the Second War, having continued for the best part of a century.

One pursuit that persisted illegally was cockfighting. I had it on the best authority, many years ago that it went on till the 1930s, despite the fact that it had been illegal since 1849. At one time, it is said, cockfighting went on in the loft of the stables of the Horse and Farrier Inn, now the house adjoining the shop, as well as in the attics of Natland Hall. The small circular walled-in wood near St. Mark's Home once concealed a cockpit.

VILLAGE INNS

Many years ago there were three inns in Natland parish, the Grey Horse, the Horse and Farrier, and the Station Inn. The Horse and Farrier figures frequently in Natland's story. For many years this very old house, now called Natland House, has been the village shop and Post Office. The Horse and Farrier is mentioned in Parson and White's Directory of 1829: at that time Jane Dawson was the 'victualler.' By 1851 the Inn was kept by Daniel Dickinson, a shoemaker and mender, and his wife Agnes. I have been unable to find out the names of later innkeepers. In 1821 the *Gentleman's*

Daniel Dickinson and his wife Agnes taken in 1880s.
Courtesy Graham Needham

Magazine reported that at Natland 'the pot-house is crowded with drunkards altho' the chapel is not more than sixteen yards distant' (p. 278). The traditional Natland Palm Fair was banned in 1835 on account of rowdy behaviour. The Inn was still plying its trade in 1885. As we have seen, the building was later bought by Jim Douthwaite, an odd-job man, who converted the adjoining stables into a house.

The Grey Horse Inn stood on the east side of what is now the A65 at Barrows Green, just north of the junction with the road that continues round 'the back of Helm;' there were also several cottages here. In 1829 Richard Proctor was 'victualler.' About this time, rather oddly, the name of the Inn was changed to Captain Ross on Clinker. The name refers to Captain Horatio Ross, a celebrated sportsman, who in March 1726, 'riding his best steeplechaser, Clinker, … beat Lord Kennedy's Radical in a match for £1000 a side;' this race was apparently regarded as the first steeplechase held in Britain (*Dictionary of National Biography*). Jacob Larwood and John Camden Hotten, in *English Inn Signs* (Exeter: Blaketon Hall, 1985) comment, 'Named riders are more rarely found, but at Natland, Westmd., over a house which has now disappeared was a figure of *Captain Ross on Clinker*. Ross was a great racing character, and gave his name to the Ross Memorial Stakes at Windsor' (p. 83). Ross's name is preserved in the nearby Ross Lodge, built some time later, by John Huck and Sons of Endmoor, for a Mr Slea, who had owned the Seven Stars in Kendal. Some of the remains of the Inn were incorporated in the new house.

Of the three Natland inns, the Station Inn, which lies right at the far north-east corner of the parish, up the hill from Oxenholme Station and facing onto Helm, is the only survivor. I haven't been able to trace the history of the Station Inn. The house and buildings appear to be old, and were probably at one time a farm. The Inn appears in Bulmer's 1885 Directory of Westmorland as 'Oxenholme Station Hotel;' George Teasdale was 'victualler' at this time. The entry in the 1906 Directory reads, 'Baker Francis Edwin, vict., Station Inn.' In 1925 the licensee was a Mr Baker. In 1930 Mr J.C. Dixon was in charge, followed by his son and family, and, until recently, his granddaughter Joyce Ormrod and her husband John. For twenty-one years the Ormrods ran a special event, the Station Inn Onion Show, in aid of charity, raising many thousands of pounds over the years (see below, 'Station Inn Onion Show'). Harry and Julie Challinor are the present licensees.

Very early picture of Station Inn at Oxenholme
(probably converted from old farm with barn still on right).

Westmorland Gazette   Courtesy Local Studies Section, Kendal Library

BEST KEPT VILLAGE

In 1987 Natland won for the second time the title of Cumbria's Best Kept Large Village; several times it has won the same title for South Lakeland.

Best Kept Village 1984
(large village section)
Kevin Noble and Pearson Charnley.
Westmorland Gazette
Courtesy Ingrid Beattie

Chapter 10

A NOTE ON FLORA AND FAUNA

Natland is lucky in having a surprising variety of wild life, both flora and fauna, in a fairly small area, depending on geology and situation. Here are a few examples.

On Helm, our local moorland, we find bracken, heather, buttercups, harebells, thyme, sorrel, stitchwort, milkwort and speedwell; trees and bushes include rowan, hawthorn, sycamore, holly, willow, birch, gorse, broom and honeysuckle. At the foot of the hill and next to the road is an area of marsh that is incredibly rich botanically, with marsh marigold, watercress, marsh pennywort, purple saxifrage, meadowsweet and two of the insectivorous plants, sundew and butterwort. In meadows and by roadsides – in their various periods of bloom – there are foxgloves, vetches, cranesbills, dog daisies, orchids, celandines, red campion, ragwort, scabious, meadow valerian, yellow-rattle, crosswort and the many lacy-flowered members of the Umbellifer family. Common weeds of cultivation include scarlet pimpernel, groundsel, docks, sorrel, shepherd's purse, thistles and plantain.

By the river we have the invasive Himalayan balsam in profusion – its seed-pods flicking their contents far and wide when ripe; actually the flowers, speckled in shades of pink, and shaped like a policeman's helmet, have a certain beauty. In woodland near the river there are some rarities – lime-loving twayblade and herb paris. Lime-loving shrubs are the spindle, with its coral-pink berries, and guelder-rose, bearing sprays of translucent 'red-jelly' berries. There were wild daffodils in the fields at one time, largely lost as a result of wartime ploughing. The woods have sheets of lovely blue wild hyacinths (bluebells), as well as wild daffodils and white-flowered wild garlic (ramsons). Ferns grow luxuriantly in woods and hedgerows, and mosses deck the old stone walls. In the autumn we have an extraordinary variety of fungi, some of them colourful, and mushrooms can be found in the fields. The ash, characteristic of limestone areas, is abundant.

Many of our wild animals are secretive and rarely seen. There are roe deer and the small muntjac in the woods, the occasional red deer, foxes, hares, weasels, stoats, and moles. Rabbits have made a comeback after the depredations of myxomatosis. John Atkinson has recently seen otters while fishing in the river. At one time we could rely on seeing red squirrels about in the woods, but they have now disappeared, and grey squirrels have taken over. There are badgers, but one would be lucky to espy them as they are nocturnal creatures. Also nocturnal, of course, are the bats, flitting through the twilight. There are frogs and toads, and there has been the odd report of a snake – whether grass-snake or adder. Hedgehogs, useful in eating garden slugs, are numerous. Recently there have even been reports of unidentified large black cats!

We have a wide variety of birds – in their different habitats – buzzards, sparrow-hawks, kestrels, owls; red grouse, curlew, lapwing, skylark, heron, and, by the river, swans, various kinds of duck, dippers and kingfishers. A skein of wild geese flying over – their call evocative of the wild – is a common sight. We also see various kinds of gulls, heading for the fells, where they feed on caterpillars, in the morning, and returning to the Kent estuary in the evening. There are the usual members of the crow family – and pigeons. Magpies, 'smart Alecs' though they are, have few friends. At one time we had corncrakes, especially in Natland Park fields: they disappeared about 1952, seemingly due to mechanisation on the farm. One has now to go to the Outer Hebrides to hear them. The garden birds include thrushes, blackbirds, sparrows, wrens, starlings, chaffinches and other finches; we have had the occasional visit of the colourful goldfinch and waxwing. And of course, there are the swifts, swallows and house martins, which we welcome each spring.

In 1970 Grassgarth, the Natland home of Captain J.C. Maples and his late wife Mrs. Enid Maples, was bequeathed to the Lake District Naturalists' Trust, an adjoining field, which was to be maintained as a bird sanctuary. The Maples had been keen members of RSPB for many years. The field is now mature woodland.

Chapter 11

CUSTOMS, SONGS AND SUPERSTITIONS

THE GYPSIES AND NATLAND PALM FAIR

The Natland gypsies, who hold an important place in the village's history, are understood to have been members of the Fa (or Faa) Gang, a tribe of gypsies who occupied an area of Scotland and northern England. Natland was their centre in this area. An article in the *Lonsdale Magazine* of 1821 describes them as 'potters.' They didn't in fact make pots: they were itinerant dealers in earthenware, making regular excursions to the Midland pottery towns to collect their wares. The gypsies, we are told, were dark and rough-looking. The women wore gaudy gowns bunched up behind to show their faded blue petticoats, their black hair was covered by a gaudy kerchief and topped by an old faded hat, and they smoked clay pipes. The women looked after their children as they walked the countryside, visiting villages and farms, selling their pots and oddments such as ribbons and lace, all carried in a basket balanced on top of their hats. They also told fortunes. The men, on the other hand, were lazy loungers, and, according to one report, good only for reproductive activities. The gypsies had been granted leave to winter in Natland in the reign of George III (1760-1820). The *Lonsdale Magazine* of 1822 reported that about eight years previously a range of buildings in which the potters resided was burnt down, and as a result they were dispersed into different parts of the village. In the census of 1851 two of the families were called Howard, one member being a baker.

The gypsies played a large part in Natland's Palm Fair. The origins of the Palm Fair are unknown, but a few details have been gleaned from various sources. In 1868 a Mr T. Blezard, formerly of Ings near Windermere, published a book, 'Original Westmorland Songs Chiefly Relating to Scenes and Incidents in the Districts of Kendal,' a copy of which Wendy Balmer kindly lent me. Of Natland Palm Fair he tells us:

> This Fair was discontinued about the year 1835. Curious to relate, it was held on Palm Sunday, latterly on that day alone, and merely as a meeting place to which Kendal people and those of the neighbourhood around used to take a walk, stroll round the village, and partake of a pot of the hostess's noted nut-brown ale. Formerly it was held several days, and embraced racing, leaping, wrestling, dancing, cock-fighting, and all other amusements common to the neighbourhood, but does not appear to have ever been chartered for cattle and chapmen's wares. At the time mentioned in the song 'Bonny Jane of Natland,' the country around was one of flocks and

herds, shepherds and herdsmen and, with the exception of the boundaries around the parks, was nearly without fences. The parks were numerous – Natland, Levens, Larkrigg, Sizergh, Brigsteer, Cunswick, and Kendal had each their parks. In the 16th and 17th Centuries, Natland was noted as the residence of several itinerant earthenware dealers, and the camping ground of numerous sojourners of that calling – as many as a dozen tents on the Green were not unusual.

Blezard does not tell us when and why the gypsies left Natland Green. Leave the Green they certainly did, though some families of their descendants camped periodically on Little Helm for many years. I remember them coming to the village, telling fortunes and selling small household goods. There were complaints about the mess they left, but I think the gypsies were not solely responsible: Little Helm had for many years been used as a public convenience for passing motorists. As I have already mentioned, Nurse Thornborrow thought highly of the gypsies. In later years they were only allowed three nights per stopping place. They would move up to Paddy Lane for a night, before returning to Little Helm, which must have been hard for them. Many years ago Little Helm was walled off in order to prevent the gypsies from camping there. Many Natland people missed their annual visit.

NB: The spelling does vary between Bonny and Bonnie – dependant on its author.

'BONNY JANE OF NATLAND'

Here are the words of the song, "Bonny Jane of Natland", as recorded by Blezard, to be sung to the tune 'Up o'er the moorlands merrily:'

Natland Fair shall be my song,
Long ago when time was young,
Then a blithesome, merry throng
Held Palm Fair at Natland;
Palms were round the village borne,
Palms the dwellings did adorn,
Crowds assembled round the Thorn
On the Green at Natland. (CR: company repeat last two lines)

Lovely Jane he chanc'd to see,
Dancing round the Hawthorn Tree.'
On the Green at Natland! (CR)

Kindly he address'd the maid,
Lovingly to her he said –
"Be not angry nor afraid

Bonny Jane of Natland"
Do not, fair one, frown on me,
If I sit me down with thee
Underneath the Hawthorn Tree
On the Green at Natland!" (CR)

"That depends, dear sir" said she,
"On your own civility.
This is called the Lover's Tree,
On the Green at Natland;
Underneath its shady boughs
Lovers oft have made their vows.
Sit you down, sir, if you choose,
On the Green at Natland!" (CR)

"Yes, I'll sit me down" said John,
"Underneath the Lover's Thorn.
Tell me, tell me, lovely one,
Bonny Jane of Natland!
Could'st thou love a shepherd's life?
Could'st thou love to hear me pipe?
Wilt thou be my loving wife,
Bonny Jane of Natland?" (CR)

"That can't be," quoth she, "kind sir,
I must ramble here and there,
Trav'ling with my earthen ware,
Still my home at Natland.
Natland is our native place,
Many of our jolly race
Here have lived to end their days –
Gone to rest at Natland!" (CR)

"List, O, listen", thus said John,
"I can bring my flocks to roam,
Round about thy darling home,
Round the Green at Natland;
Then in peace and unity,
Happy, happy, we shall be,
Here beside the Hawthorn Tree,
On the Green at Natland!" (CR)

Before a year was past and gone
Jane was married unto John;
Long they dwelt beside the Thorn
On the Green at Natland!

Many years they lived to see
Natland Fair, and rounds of glee,
Round about the Lover's Tree,
On the Green at Natland! (CR)

The Natland subscribers to Mr Blezard's song book, incidentally, were: Miss A. Shepherd, Mrs M. Harrison, E. Cannon of Crow Park, Mr Just Jun., J. Bell, E. Gibson, J. Park, J. Summers, W. Allen of Newlands, J. Read, R. Noble of Natland Park, J. Mullard, T. Hutchinson, R. Wilson, R. Brook, E. Moorhouse, and W. Read.

'BONNY JANE:' A POSTSCRIPT

In the *Westmorland Gazette* of July 8th 1977 there appeared a letter from a Miss Elsie M. Fitzsimmons of Swarthmoor, on the outskirts of Ulverston; I believe she taught at Natland School back in the 1930s. Her letter reads:

Sir – I was most interested to read Mr Walter Jesson's letter regarding the colourful float 'Bonny Jane of Natland,' at the Jubilee Parade on Natland Green. In May, 1935, when I was secretary of the Natland Women's Institute, some of the members, trained by their very able producer, the late Mrs V.M. Keesey, of Fisherflatt, gave a delightful, original item on Natland Green, entitled 'Bonnie (sic) Jane of Natland.' The musician from Kendal Town was Mr Stan Robinson, who played his accordion. The poem I wrote was as follows:

One eve, in the merry month of May,
'Twas all upon Natland Green,
A group of maids from our W. I.,
Revived an old time scene.
In recitation, mime and dance,
They told how Bonnie Jane
Was wooed and won by Shepherd John,
From yonder Sizergh Plain.
At Natland Palm Fair once again
A jolly Potter Race
Sold earthenware and basketry,
Sweet flowers and dainty lace.
Endowed with mystic art one maid,
Told to both lass and lad,
What fortune had in store for them,
Whether 'twas good or bad.
A musician from Kendal town there came,
A player of skill was he,
And maids and swains to merry strains

Danced round the hawthorn tree.
The nut-brown ale they freely drank
To BONNIE Jane and John,
On Natland Green. One eve last May
As in days of long agone.

ANOTHER NATLAND SONG, AND TWO POEMS

I should record a song, and two comic poems intended for recitation, that Mrs Pooley Nelson dictated to me in the 1960s. By this time she was very old: her memory was not quite as good as it had been, and I think we got slightly muddled in places. The song, which was apparently sung at weddings, is 'progressive,' its farm animal theme reminiscent of 'Old Macdonald Had a Farm:'

I Bought a Cock

I bought a cock, and cock pleased me.
I fed it under the tree.
Cocky went cocky-oodly-oo,
It's well for every neighbour's cock to crow
And my cock do!
I bought a hen, and hen pleased me,
I fed it under the tree.
Hen went chicky-chuck,
Cocky went cocky-oodly-oo.........etc.
I bought a horse and horse pleased me,
I fed it under the tree,
The horse went hinny,
The cow went bo-wy,
The dog went bow-wow,
The sheep went baa-baa,
The goose went hissy,
The duck went quicky-quack,
The hen went chicky-chuck.
The cock went cocky-oodly oo,
It's well for every neighbour's cock to crow
And my cock do!

The Runaway Wedding

I'll tell you a story if willing you be
A wat in me young days once happened to me.
At yam wid mi mudder and fadder did dwell,

A was named like mi fadder – they called me Jack Brown,
A better-like chap never walked through that town.
For twenty long years our folk had been wed
And I was all't baien that ever they had
Whativer I wanted I got mi own way.
Now Dr. Thompson, mi fadder's old friend
Came to our spot for a few days to spend
And with that auld chap they cum a smart daughter
For a bit of an outing he said he had brought her.
For soon she would gang for short was her stay
And I felt like crying when she went away.
I moped about, depressed and downhearted
And all seemed amiss with mi darling departed.
But unsuspected we managed to meet,
I went acourting every Saturday neet.
Mi joys were so big mi wits near had flown
When I got her to say she'd be Mrs John Brown.
We agreed there and then next Saturday neet
Was a likely time for't moon to be leet
And I mud come ower about't hour o' three
And she'd be ready about same time as me,
And then we'd ga to a parson for our life
And afore owt could stop us we'd be made man and wife.
As I drew near I heard three striking
And from't open window I spied mi love peeping
And to her assistance I fetched a short ladder.
No mak a loud noise, you'll waken mi fadder.
Now Mary's next sister, her name it was Bess
And there by the window she did stand
Thraw us that bundle and look sharp about it
When a voice says 'What means all that talking?
And a yedand a nightcap cam poking.
We stood fixed to't spot as if bund with a spell
For we knew it was old Mr Thompson hissel.
That imp of a Bess had told him allt' plot
And he'd been at lookout 'fore I got to't spot.
He crept into't room with care and with caution
He'd heard every word and watched evert motion.
'Shouldn't tease thy sister in this way he said –
They in a hurry and going to be wed.
'And where are you going to live at, Jacky?' he cried.
'I really can't tell you' I faintly replied.
'We'll' says he,' I never heard sic a tale in y life
To run off at this time of night to be wed.

Tha's got neither money nor house nor a bed,'
And he shouted again and he laughed for his life.
Sky all the night had been owercast and cloudy
And afore long it was as light as day
With the noise that we'd med folks at windows cum peeping.
'Hey break thy neck, lad' some of them cried,
Some shouted 'Cu back with thee bundle and bride.'
Like a hare frae the hunters I fled
And I manfully stood by my vow to this day
And afoor I'll meet one I'll turn out o't way.
Now lads just take my advice
Don't meddle with't lasses though ever so nice
But first ask your mudder and o as your bid
And remember me and mi runaway wedding.

Christmas Party

When cold December breezes blow and chimney tops do rumble,
A lot of young folks smart and gay and old ones free and hearty,
Agreed among thersells that they
Wod have a Xmas party.
At yam some nete, they kicked up sek a fuss an spread
And med sik preparations,
They baked grand tarts and mixed their bread,
With spices fra all nations
To drive away both want and cold,
It seemed their inclination
And letters round both young and old,
Oh gat an invitation
To gang that neet.
Bright sprigs of ivy green were fra the ceiling hanging
And in the midst conspicuous scene the mistletoe was swinging.
The lamps shone forth as clear as day
And there was nowt neglected.
Some happy smiling faces say some company is expected
To come this neet.
And first come Moll and Gert Lang Jack
A strapping like good fellow
And at their back come Bob and Isabella.
Why how d'you and how's yursell?
Men draw their chairs up to fire and merrily passed their jokes off
While lassies, they slipped off upstairs,
To tak their hats and cloaks off.

Before a glass, that hung at side
They all take up their station
And thinks within thersells with pride they'll cause a gert sensation
Among lads this neet then to this good substantial fare
Oh got an invitation
And some with time to put it by played havoc with each dainty
While some they were so varra shy scarce lets thersells ha plenty.
Som's shouting a lile bit mare and plates and glasses rattle
And some no time a word to pass, thrang supping and thrang biting
While simmering sits a gert soft lass and waits for much inviting.
Then when this good substantial fare as given them satisfaction
They side oh chairs and stand in pairs
With heels in tune for action.
Says he te Fiddler he begins as best as he is able
He rosins sticks and screws up pins and jumps up on ta table
To play that neet
Some dance with splendid style and ease, with tightly fitted togs on
While others jump about, like drainers with their clogs on.
Then when they have reeled and danced their fling
Men drew up their chairs up to fire in earnest conversation
On ways and means of saving brass and rules and laws oh nation.
Oh women preached and talked about their clothes being old and rotten
And scarce could afford to speak a clout for seck a price was cotton.
Now Gert Lang Jack as lives at Moor with cunning and with caution
Ia begging Moll to ga to to door,
Moll taks the hint nor thinks it wrang her heart that way inclining,
She says ta rest she think she gang to see if stars is shining.
At first they tak a walk and then they wend their way back
And for a bit of pleasant talk they shelter under haystack.
She dident say neet she thow oft times Johnny kissed her
She said she would just run and see if other folks has missed her.
A chap who had two wackful eyes
On wich they woorent thinking
When looking around room catched Jack and Molly winking.
Says he nows time to have a stir
We'll have some fun if we can nobbut catch hem.
So out they went, but scarce could see. It was as dark as dungeon.
Jack hears their footsteps coming slow and fra her side he slenks off,
Runs around house end, jumps ower wall,
And up to knees in sink trough.
Now you lads where ere you be, don't do owt in a stutter,
But learn to look before you leap,
Lest you in some deep gutter stick fast some neet.

Natland's Dobbies

What goings-on! Well into the nineteenth century belief in ghosts and hauntings was widespread. This account of the Natland 'dobbies' appeared in the *Lonsdale Magazine* of December 1821:

The principal dobby is the one in the following tale – a man and his wife once lived at Natland, but not being on the best of terms – the wife poisoned the husband and the husband, to reward her for her kindness, afterwards haunted her. The immaterial husband now got the better of the material wife, and often, what he could never do in his lifetime, beat her black and blue. This treatment soon brought the wife likewise to her grave, to the no small consolation of the villagers who now naturally imagined that the dobby would be quiet. In this however, they were mistaken; for lo! After the funeral, instead of one dobby there were, afterwards, two. The strangest sights were now seen in the house – the most unaccountable sounds were heard. Even during the day the noise of quarrelling was heard as usual and the same sound of blows. In the night lights were seen in the rooms. In consequence, the road passing the house was almost deserted, the villagers durst not attend the chapel because of its near neighbourhood to the haunted house. This induced the parson of the parish to enquire into the matter, who, convinced of the truth of the statement, determined upon the dobby's expulsion; and, went through all the established forms of exorcism, he led his captives to Hawes Bridge, and there 'laid' the dobbies in the trough beneath – 'long as the ivy above them should be green.' They, however, occasionally escaped. One of them again visits the village, where it spends the short time it is allowed its liberty in spinning in the garret of its favourite house. It is known in Natland as 'Kittle my belly.' The other dobby amuses itself about the bridge, in stopping up stiles and terrifying midnight passengers. So beware!   (p.459)

There is also a reference to 'the versi-coloured rabbit of Scit Scot Brow.' The name conjures up a picture of Scots rebels fleeing in great disarray up Oxenholme Lane or Helm Lane. Could this be some kind of folk memory of the brightly clothed Bonnie Prince Charlie? Other 'dobbies' mentioned in the article are: Old Minikin the miser, who drowned himself in the 'dub' to prevent himself from being starved; the White Lady of Smallthorn's Stile; the Grinning Human Head in Natland Park's Yeat Stoup; the Headless Man who pursued people with his detached head, 'from the last turn in Elsey Lane to Salt Pie Hall;' and the White Cat of 'Crakelt Lane head.' A large black dobby with its winding sheet was to be glimpsed at the Tithe Barn End. On Helm, by the Haunted Stone, where a murdered lady was said to be buried, one might see a head beset with large branching horns rise out of the stone itself, while twelve human hands set down twelve lighted candles beside it. In 'Lakerigg' there were the 'bloody one at Well Parrock Yeat,' and the white combed cock of Cock Crow's Corner. Further afield, there were the Force Bridge Dobby in Sedgwick, the Invisible Hand in Pig Willy Wood, and the Mastiff of Shyrakes Brow. Natland people certainly seem to have been extremely superstitious: one suspects that Mrs Dawson's celebrated brown ale was too much of a good thing.

SOME OLD CUSTOMS

Various customs were observed right up to the beginning of the last War, but only one, apparently, has survived through to the present day – that of wishing at the Wishing Tree on Helm. I wonder how many generations of children have done this, and when did it start? Doubtless there has been a succession of trees. The old Wishing Tree was a huge spreading sycamore which stood at the back of the high field wall, bordering the south-west corner of Helm, by the path leading to the lane round 'the back of Helm.' Some years ago the old tree was felled – or did it blow down? – and a sapling sycamore was planted in its place.

The Wishing Tree
Courtesy late Mrs. Maple

The custom is to find a small stone, spit on it whilst making a silent wish, and insert it in a crevice of the wall beneath the over-hanging branches of the tree – that is, if you can find an empty crevice. So laden with the stones does the wall become that, at intervals of several years, it falls down. The owner of the field builds the wall up again, and the Wishing Tree custom starts again. Natland children have a proven place to register their need for a doll's pram, a new bike or whatever.

It is difficult to explain why other customs have disappeared. Well into the twentieth century, 'pace' eggs were rolled on Easter Sunday down a hill at Cracalt. On Ascension Day, or 'Spanish Water Day' as the children knew it, all took bottles of liquorice and water to School: these were shaken till bubbles and froth arose, then surreptitiously drunk. Usually the teacher tried to locate the bottles, and would line them up till playtime. One explanation of this custom was that the rising bubbles represented the

Ascension. There are records of similar children's customs involving 'Spanish Water' or 'Spanish Juice' elsewhere in Cumberland and Westmorland. In Natland a daisy was worn on a particular day, though no one, apparently, knew why: in some places this custom was observed on Empire Day. At Easter the village was invaded by a noisy band of 'Jolly Boys' from Kendal, dressed in weird costumes and touring the village, banging tin lids and shouting the words, 'Trot herring, trot on – Good Friday to morn' – or what sounded like this. I read somewhere that this custom probably marked the end of Lent. Some of the smaller children were scared by these noisy antics.

NATLAND TREACLE MINES

There is a traditional joke about the 'Natland treacle mines.' According to a recently published book, Jennifer Westwood and Jacqueline Simpson, *The Lore of the Land: A Guide to England's Legends* (London: Penguin, 2005), there are about thirty places in England boasting treacle mines, most of which carry similar explanations. The Natland entry runs:

In the year 1211, a man searching for Roman treasures in a cavern saw an ancient pot apparently filled with gold, guarded by a snake. Recklessly he seized it; the snake bit him, his hand began to swell and throb, and he fainted, breaking the pot. But what it held was a golden syrup, which cured his hand at once. Knowing that this was more precious than any coins, the man explored the cave and found a spring of treacle. For centuries this has brought health and wealth to the villagers, but no outsider is ever told where the golden spring may be.   (p. 715)

I have had a long association with Natland, and have never heard this story. There may be a less fanciful explanation for the tradition. At one time there was a sawpit opposite Compton House, roughly where, until recently, the Wellingtonia tree grew. With a pair of staunch sawyers operating a cross-cut saw, working on pine, a quantity of sticky resin might have accumulated, bearing some resemblance to golden syrup or treacle. This is, of course, just guesswork.

Chapter 12

MISCELLANY

CARE OF THE VILLAGE GREEN

During the Civil War (1642-48), Natland's Lord of the Manor was living in exile, and the Sizergh estates were broken up. Since the end of the Stuart period, the Lords of the Manor have retained only manorial rights in Natland, which include ownership of the Green. The Parish Council, which maintains the Green, has applied to take it over, but so far without success.

PLAYING FIELDS

From time to time the Parish Council has made efforts to find a playing field, but so far in vain: otherwise suitable fields are too near housing or simply too expensive. The School, however, has an excellent playing field, and children are allowed to play there during holidays. Oxenholme has a good playground for younger children. There is a fine swimming pool at Kendal Leisure Centre, at the southern end of the town, and all the secondary schools have sports grounds: so children have plenty of opportunity to participate in physical activities.

VERMIN!

It is recorded that in 1681 Kendal Churchwardens were paying the following rewards for catching vermin: otter 6d, 'brocke' (badger) 6d, wild cat 4d. The vermin heads had to be presented with hair still on; afterwards they were thrown into the river. At Underbarrow a fox head brought no less than 12d.

A DANCING BEAR

Mrs Dixon of Sedgwick, who was born in Natland and spent her childhood here, told me that a dancing bear, which performed to the accompaniment of a hurdy-gurdy, occasionally made an appearance in the village. The children had to take a penny – or was it a halfpenny? – to watch the bear performing. Mrs Dixon didn't know where the bear and its master came from. They must have walked, the man trundling the hurdy-gurdy along: where would they sleep at night? It must have been a punishing life for both master and bear.

AU PAIRS

Au-pair girls were a solution to a shortage of household help. Mrs Maples of Grassgarth had a series of Danish au pairs, who helped as necessary in return for their keep and pocket money. They came to further their education, many of them being students, and they made friends in the village. In about 1960 Bodil Kjaer was often at our house in her free time. On one occasion we took Bodil and another Danish au pair up Helvellyn. Bodil came back to see us some years later after she was married.

THE WELLINGTONIA

Until recently there was a magnificent Wellingtonia tree (Sequoiadendron Giganteum) on the corner of the village Green opposite Compton House. Unfortunately it had to be felled, as it was obviously in decline. The reason for its slow death is not clear. According to the *Collins Field Guide to Trees*, wellingtonias occasionally die from root-fungus. Perhaps weedkiller played a part. Audrey Ireland examined the cut surface and counted the tree-rings – about 166 – indicating the approximate age of the tree.

EARTHQUAKES

Natland experiences occasional earthquakes. Several notable ones occurred in the Kendal area in the seventeenth century. I remember one in the 60s, and the most recent was in September 1988, with its epicentre near Ambleside.

VILLAGE PEACE SHATTERED BY NOISE

There has always been the occasional interruption of Natland's quiet. The *Westmorland Gazette* of Nov. 26th 1976 carried the front-page headline 'Motorbikes Shatter a Village's Peace.' Several of the local teenage population, together with youths from other villages and Kendal, congregated on Natland Green, spending much of their time revving up their motorbikes. The hawthorn tree was damaged, and there was a muddy mess around the seat, with much litter. One resident whose house faced onto the Green complained to the Police and the Parish Council; but Mrs Ruth Holmes, of Green View, took the view that the youths were not vandals, just youngsters with nowhere else to go. The problem apparently solved itself, and there was no more trouble.

MAKE DO AND MEND

During and for some time after the last War, we had clothing coupons, which forced us to be careful of clothing, and encouraged us to do mending, and actually make what garments we could. This entailed a good deal of extra work for mothers. We did a lot of 'passing down' of outgrown items within the family, including near relations, as well as among friends. Sometimes we were able to make new items from the better parts of an old garment. One small boy went to School proudly announcing that his new jacket and pants were made from Aunty So-and-So's mother's best coat. Today's children are turned out in the latest children's fashion, and I don't think there will be much mending and making-do. Doting Grandmas still do knitting for their grandchildren, when they have time between all the things modern Grandmas do.

CHEAP MEALS

Miss Miller once lent me a little booklet that had been published by Titus Wilson of Kendal in 1909. It was called 'The Kendal Penny Cookery Book,' and was used by the Borough Education Committee for use in Elementary School cookery classes for girls. The book contained a number of plain recipes. There were ideas for 'penny dinners' for six people, such as: 2 quarts of pea soup at 3d, suet dumplings at 2½d, syrup at ½d, the total cost being 6d – 1d per person! There were also suggestions for a whole week of cheap meals, but I notice the Sunday dinner would run out more expensively: 4 pounds beef at 3s 4d, Yorkshire pudding at 4d, baked or roast potatoes at 2d, and rice pudding at 2d – at a total cost of 4s, which would surely be too large a slice of the week's wage for many households.

BURIALS IN WOOLLEN

In 1678 the Burials in Woollen Act stated that corpses had to be buried in a woollen shroud. Relatives had to obtain an affidavit from the minister or magistrate proving that they had complied with this regulation, or else they faced a fine. This measure was to encourage the wool trade. In 1684 William Barrow of Natland was 'buryed in Linnen,' but no more was heard of it. The Act was repealed in 1814.

SOME ITEMS FROM THE LOCAL NEWSPAPERS,
THE KENDAL MERCURY AND WESTMORLAND GAZETTE

1825 Jan. 8th: 'Wm. Wakefield has improved Larkrigg Dam, near Sedgwick, so as to render passage for the salmon up the river less difficult.'

Letter to Kendal Mercury, 1843: 'When the Pretender was in Kendal he was quartered on Thomas Shepherd, of a family of Natland, the last male representative of which was the father of Mrs W.C. Wilson of Casterton Hall.'

[no date]: 'A disgraceful riot arose on Sunday out of a football match amongst the young men of the townships of Killington, Natland and Hutton. The ball was driven towards this town, fences and crops were destroyed, and it being finally carried off by one of the Natland party, their

outraged opponents pursued them, and fighting and violent outrage occurred in various parts of the town. It is much to be regretted that the constitution of our statutes respecting the violations of the Sabbath is such as to make it difficult to convict the offenders.'

1826: John Carradice, of Natland, killed by lightning in Birkrigg Park, near Kendal.

1830: 'At a chapel not a hundred miles from Natland, we are informed that the whole congregation last Sunday consisted of the officiating clergyman, clerk and church-warden.'

ALTAR FRONTAL

The Natland Parish Magazine of February 1976, during Canon Westropp's incumbency, contained the following item:

> Some time ago, Canon R. Waddington, of Carlisle, was visiting St. Mark's Church, Natland. He noticed the red velvet altar frontal and immediately recognised the material as being identical in design to vestments – a set of copes – used at the Coronation of Edward VII in Westminster Abbey. It is believed that some of this material was made available to churches at the time, 1901, and it is possible that the frontal was first used in the 'new' St. Mark's in 1910. Until Canon Waddington's visit, no one had realised the value and significance of the frontal, which was in a rather shabby state. But action was taken!

> Canon Westropp had the super-frontal re-appliqued SANCTUS SANCTUS SANCTUS in London, and whilst there, it was loaned to the B.B.C. for use in a television programme on church embroidery. For the repair of the main frontal Canon Westropp called upon the skill of Mrs Clara Ball, Waterfield, Natland. Mrs Ball found it necessary to remove most of the gold thread and re-work and oversew it with new, a conservative estimate of the time taken being 170/180 hours. A mammoth task indeed, for which the parishioners of St. Mark's are extremely grateful. Due to her 'labour of love' and Canon Westropp's prompt action, St. Mark's owns a beautiful altar frontal.

STATION INN ONION SHOW

The *Westmorland Gazette* for September 29th 1989 reported the last of the Station Inn Onion shows:

Success for last onions

Sunday's last-ever onion show at the Station Inn, Oxenholme, has broken all previous records by raising around £4,000 for charity. This year's show – the 21st of its kind – was described as 'the end of an era' by organisers, who have decided it should be the last. Mr George Bell, who regularly helped judge the entries, died recently and donations from his funeral went towards this year's charities – Cancer Care and the Lancaster Scanner Appeal. Show chairman Mr Peter Hull said 'We have had a lot of fun over the years and now we have decided to call it a day. I would like on behalf of the Station Inn to thank everyone who has supported us. I also want to thank Joyce and John Ormrod, licensees of the Station Inn, for letting us hold it there.

The show began when Lancastrian, Peter Hull and Yorkshireman, Frank Emmett could not agree who grew the best onions. They settled the argument by showing them in the pub, and this very first show raised just £12. In 1989 Mr Hull's six-hour auction made £2,300, with donations and the proceeds of a raffle have taking the total to around £4,000. One of the items in the auction was of special interest to sports fans: former England and Worcester cricketer Basil D'Oliveira, a friend of Mr Hull, donated a cricket bat autographed by that year's Australian Tourists and the England 11. It raised £160. The Cherry Cup for the best exhibit in the show went to Mrs Sheila Ormrod, the licensee's daughter-in-law. The set of three champion onions was auctioned off for £21. The show attracted twenty-five exhibits – slightly up on the previous year. The judges were John and Joyce Ormrod. The results were: Cherry Cup for best exhibit, Mrs Sheila Ormrod; W. Walling Cup for housewives' choice, Mrs Sheila Ormrod; Whitbread Cup for best local exhibit, 1 Mrs L. Teasdale, 2 Louise and Paul, 3 Mr Morgan; housewives' choice, 1 Mrs S. Ormrod, 2 Mrs C. Middleton, 3 Mrs I. Marriner.

MRS HAMER'S MEMORIES OF NATLAND

[Enid Hamer was Mrs Cartmell's cousin, and wrote these notes for me].

Rose Cottage and the adjoining cottage now called Dalegarth, leased by my grandfather, Benjamin Tyson Porter, in 1868 on returning to native country, with wife and baby son (who was my father), from Burton-on Trent. He bought the cottages in 1885 from Carus Wilson – also rented orchard behind cottages along the road to south where Home Lea now stands. Rose Cottage then much as Dalegarth now is (1955) – only a living room and two bedrooms – one of which led from the other. Grandfather died 1907 or 8 – five children – to accommodate these he enlarged cottage himself – added parlour with bedroom above. On N. side of cottage there were a wash-house and a heated greenhouse with a prolific grape-vine, now both gone. There was also a pig-sty in a little yard between the cottage garden and the Abbey orchard and at the N. end there was a privy serving both cottages. Also kept hens in the little yard. Also had a supplementary garden opp. The Church. (where Tithe Barn was?) The lane was much narrower then. The Rev. W. gave Latin and Greek lessons to my father before school on summer mornings. The other cottage was occupied by a widow, Mrs Smart, who took in washing from bigger houses.

The old Church was narrow and bare, with hanging oil lamps. Home boys came to church in thick capes of navy-blue cloth and carrying lanterns which were left in the porch – parishioners from distant houses also carried lanterns.

There was a shop, and in my very early childhood, a public house about where the P.O. now stands. In shop very few packet goods – hams and bacon, flour and oatmeal in large open-necked sacks standing on the floor and other sacks containing provender and Indian corn. At door of one of the cottages on Kendal Rd would sit an old woman smoking a pipe.

In the kitchen of Natland Hall – a plant grew out of floor and twined round grandfather clock – they called it a 'tray' (tea) plant– one of these on my garden wall – another name for it 'Duke of Argyll's tea plant.' Oxenholme Lane was known as Shannie's Lane. He (Nathaniel Hutchinson) had his farm there, (now Greenside) – he kept a pony and trap for hire to and from station. Only transport in Natland then horsedrawn and private – people always walked to Kendal for shopping. Grandfather B.T.P. worked on railway. Some worked on farms and at powder works at Sedgwick – two of latter, Sill and Benson, lived at cottages below High House – now Armer's.

Pace-egging on Easter Monday on smooth steep field on other side of railway or on lower slopes of Helm. There was also 'Spanish Water Day' which fell on November 5th. Children delighted in the echo in a sammle quarry on the side of Helm. My father and his brother would steal fog signals from cabins by the side of the railway to smoke out wasps' nests – or capture a fowl, climb onto the roof of one of the farms and drop the bird down the chimney. There were many mushrooms in fields and watercress was gathered in Watery Lane between Cracalt and the canal.   E.H.

I hope you have enjoyed reading about Natland and share with me my wish, that it remains as such, for future generations to love and enjoy as I have done!

Kendal Corn Rent Map 1836 – Plan of Township of Natland (large extract).

Courtesy Graham Needham

OWNERS AND TENANTS

The manuscript schedule for the Kendal Corn Rent map of 1836 tells us much about the field pattern and field use at this time. The fields are numbered, but not in numerical order. Names of owners are indicated by capitals, while those of tenants appear in lower-case:

MR BULLFIELD
No.3, Sarah Bullfield, cottage, barn and garden
38, himself, public house and orchard (later Horse & Farrier Inn)
ADAM ASKEW, Esq.
181, William Sim, Slaythornes
MR BINLEY
5, Jas. Grime, orchard
MRS BURTON
27, Wm. Creighton, homestead (now Greenside)
30, ... barn and paddock (barn opposite Greenside)
57, ... – pasture
58, ... – meadow
59, ... – pasture – 2 acres
111, ... – pasture – 3 acres
112, ... Watery Pasture – 4 acres
118, ... – meadow – 7 acres
119, ... – meadow
121, ... Stripes – pasture
147, ... – arable – 1 acre
152, ... – pasture – 3 acres
28, ...
129, ...
ADAM ASKEW
177, Wm. Simm, Highfield – pasture – 6 acres
180, ... Low Highfield – pasture – 6 acres
196, ... Chamber Ings – meadow – 8 acres

198, ... Old Natland – pasture – 8 acres
199, ... High Sattery – arable – 3 acres
201, ... Orchard (Watercrook)
202, ... High Crook – meadow – 8 acres
203, ... Low Crook – meadow – 8 acres
204, ... Barn Close – meadow – 5 acres
205, ... House and homestead (Watercrook)
206, ... Horse Close – pasture – 4 acres
207, ... Sattery – arable – 8 acres
208, ... Pots Land – meadow – 3 acres
213, ... Willy Field – arable – 6 acres
WM. BAINBRIDGE
277, himself, Orchard and garden (Newlands)
278, ... – 1 acre
289, ... – pasture – 2 acres
290, ... – meadow – 2 acres
291, ... – meadow – 2 acres
292, ... & others, Houses (Newlands)
MR BARROW
159, Carr – meadow – 3 acres
160, ... – meadow – 3 acres
162, Jas. Webster, Natland Beck Meadow – meadow – 5 acres
164, ... Natland Beck Meadow – meadow –1 acre
165, ... Road
167, ... Mill Close – pasture – 2 acres
MRS CASTLEHOW
78, Herself & J. Brock, Cottages & orchards

D. CRUDESON Esq.
153, John Atkinson, Holling Close – arable – 4 acres
156, ... Great Wars (Graham's field) – arable & meadow – 5 acres
157, ... – meadow – 4 acres
168, ... House, homestead & garden (Natland Millbeck)
169, ... Plantation – wood
170, ... Mill Floor – meadow – 7 acres
171, ... Plantation – wood
172, ... Shepherd Eagle (Horse Field) – meadow – 4 acres
173, ... Far Horse Field – arable & meadow – 4 acres
178, ... Natland Field – arable & meadow – 5 acres
184, ... – pasture – 7 acres
187, ... Millfield – pasture – 10 acres
192, ... Mill Paddock – meadow – 1 acre
166, ... Plantations – wood
182, ... Slaythornes – pasture – 2 acres
183, ... Plantation – wood
185, ... Garden (Helme Lodge Garden) – 2 acres
186, ... Garden – 1 acre
188, ... Plantation – wood
189, ... Plantation – wood
190, ... Plantation – wood
191, ... Plantation – wood

CHARITY SCHOOL
155, Jas. Webster, Charity Field – meadow – 2 acres

CHAPEL AND YARD
17

CANAL COMPANY
193, John Jackson, Mill Paddock – meadow
194, ... Mill Yard etc.
195, themselves, Plantation – wood
212, ... Canal – 8 acres
.... Banks – 3 acres

MR GIBSON
Himself and others, Blacksmith's shop and cottage

JAMES GRAHAM
38a, Himself and others, Cottages (Park Cottages)

MRS HALHEAD
28, Wm. Creighton
129, ... – 1 acre

MR FAWCETT
88, Richard Proctor – pasture – 3 acres
89, ... – pasture – 1 acre
.... Plantation in above – wood
92, ... Notts Hill – arable – 1 acre
93, ... – meadow – 5 acres
96, ... Orchard
97a, ... Yard, house and homestead
105, ... – pasture
106, ... – pasture – 2 acres
107, ... – arable – 4 acres
108, ... – arable – 4 acres
281, ... – meadow – 6 acres
97, George Watson, House and garden
93, ... Stable and orchard
131, J. Fawcett – 2 acres
132, W. Bainbridge – arable – 2 acres
132a, J. Fawcett – 1 acre
133, ... – 1 acre

DR HOLMES
246, Bessy Shepherd, Cock Crow – arable – 3 acres
247, ... 4-Acre – meadow – 5 acres
248, ... Barn Close – meadow – 3 acres
249, ... Briary Brow – arable
254, ... Reddins – arable – 3 acres
255, ... – arable – 1 acre
256, ... – pasture – 2 acres

257, ... – pasture – 1 acre
258, ... – pasture – 3 acres
263, ... Pease Close – pasture – 3 acres
267, ... Orchard (Cracalt)
268, ... House, homestead etc. (Cracalt)
269, ... Garden (Cracalt)
270, ... Paddock (Cracalt)

C. JOHNSON Esq.
99, Richard Herdson, Public House & garden (The Grey Horse, B. Green)
100, ... Orchard
101, ... Orchard
102, ... – pasture – 2 acres
103, ... – arable
104, ... – pasture – 3 acres
282, ... – meadow – 4 acres
283, ... Plantation – wood
284, ... – meadow – 2 acres
285, ... – arable – 2 acres
286, ... – pasture – 2 acres
287, ... – pasture – 2 acres
288, ... – meadow – 3 acres
94, ... – meadow – 3 acres
95, ... Paddock – pasture
95a, ... Homestead

WM. WILSON
145, J. Manzergh – pasture – 10 acres

POOR OF UNDERMILL BECK
174, J. Just – arable – 6 acres

POOR OF WINDERMERE
264, J. Just, Willread field (Little Cracalt) – arable – 1 acre
265, ... Garden (Little Cracalt) – arable

MR RAVEN
2a, Mary Birkett, Cottage and garden

JOHN ROBINSON Esq.
295, John Murray, Far Newlands –pasture – 8 acres
296, ... High Pengill – arable – 4 acres
297, ... House Close – pasture – 7 acres
298, ... Orchard
299, ... Meadow – meadow – 4 acres
300, ... Horse Close –arable – 4 acres
301, ... Nanny Sil – meadow – 1 acre
302, ... Middle Field – arable – 4 acres

THOS. STRICKLAND Esq.
1 Natland Green
32, Thos. Harrison, Little Lound – arable – 8 acres
36, ... Parrock
37, ... Road to the Parks
39, ... Orchard and road
40, ... Great Lound – pasture – 13 acres
41, ... Stony Park – arable – 15 acre
42, ... Part of 16-acre – arable – 9 acres
43, ... Part of 16-acres – arable – 11 acres
44, ... House, homestead and orchard (Natland Park)
45, ... The Lime-kiln Field – pasture – 8 acres
46, ... Near Bank – arable – 6 acres
47, ... Far Bank – pasture – 10 acres
50, ... Buck Well Park – arable – 12 acres
51, ... Watery Field – arable – 9 acres

REV. STRICKLAND
238, J. Just, Low Fields – arable – 7 acres
239, ... Low Fields – arable & meadow – 2 acres
240, ... Low Fields – pasture – 1 acre

W. W. C. WILSON Esq.
4, Elizabeth Read, House, homestead and orchard (Natland Hall)
6, ... Orchard
11, ... Paddock – pasture
33, ... Barn and paddock – meadow

48, ... Short Park Side (Claphams Field) – meadow – 7 acres
79, ... Robert Lee Field – meadow and arable – 9 acres
117, ... Reddins – pasture –10 acres
176, ... Long Park Side – arable – 6 acres
179, ... Broad Flatt –arable – 8 acres
200, ... Waste and plantation – wood
209, ... Plantation (Bank Side) – wood
210, ... Plantation (Bank Side) – wood
211, ... Beckfield End – meadow – 4 acres
215, ... Top of Long Field – meadow – 7 acres
216, ... Far Long Field – seeds – 4 acres
217, ... Second Long Field – meadow – 7 acres
218, ... First Long Field – arable and meadow – 9 acres
218a, ... Plantation – wood
219, ... Fitz – arable – 10 acres
220, ... Ring Field – meadow – 9 acres
221, ... Little Ring Field – seeds – 1 acre
222, ... Lime Kiln Field – pasture – 9 acres
223, ... Great Yeats – pasture – 3 acres
224, ... Yeat Stoops – pasture – 10 acres
225, ... Busky Sloes – arable – 3 acres
226, ... Bottom Close – seeds – 6 acres
226, ... Plantation in above – wood
227, ... Low Dyehouse – seeds – 3 acres
228, ... Low Grubbins – arable – 2 acres
229, ... Grubbins – arable – 2 acres
259, Elizabeth Read, Barn Close – pasture – 2 acres
279, ... High Field – arable – 1 acre
7, Jonathan Just, House, homestead and orchard (Town End)
8, ... Paddock – pasture
9, ... – 4 acres
260, ... Jennet – meadow – 3 acres
261, ... Birket – pasture – 3 acres
262, ... Raise – meadow – 4 acres

262, ... Plantation in above – wood
266, ... Croft – meadow – 1 acre
271, ... Far Field – arable and meadow – 8 acres
272, ... Plantation in above – wood
273, ... Middle Field – arable – 6 acres
276, ... Craycolt Croft – pasture – 5 acres
10, ... New Field – pasture – 6 acres
James Morris, Tam Close – meadow –3 acres
12, ... (and another) Houses, homestead & gardens (N. Abbey)
14, ... Orchard
15, ... Paddock – pasture
16, ... – meadow – 2 acres
18, ... School Paddock – arable
19, ... School and garden
25, ... Paddock – pasture
61, ... Barrel Know – arable – 2 acres
64, ... Kemp Field – seeds – 5 acres
66, ... – pasture –2 acres
67, ... – arable – 2 acres
68, ... – arable – 3 acres
69, ... – pasture – 5 acres
72, ... – pasture – 4 acres
73, ... – arable – 5 acres
80, ... Clemmet Orchard – meadow – 3 acres
115, ... Fell Close – pasture – 7 acres
128, ... Little Reddins – arable – 3 acres
275, ... Middle Field – arable – 3 acres
13, John Cloudsdale, Cottage & garden (used to be Cartmell's)
23, J. Bell & E. Read, Cottage, barn & orchard
24, ... Garden (Low House)
26, Jas. Webster, Kemp Paddock – pasture – 1 acre
29, ... House, Homestead & 2 orchards (Higher House)
31, ... Low Paddock – pasture – 1 acre
49, ... Top of Elsy Lane – arable – 6 acres